Why You Should

Tom Ramey, Director, DB2 for z/OS
IBM Silicon Valley Laboratory

"This book is a 'must read' for Enterprise customers and contains a wealth of valuable information!

"It is clear that there is a technology paradigm shift underway, and this is opening enormous opportunities for companies in all industries. Adoption of Cloud, Mobile, and Analytics promises to revolutionize the way we do business and will add value to a company's business processes across all functions from sales, marketing, procurement, manufacturing and finance.

"IT will play a significant role enabling this shift. Read this book and find out how to integrate the heart of your infrastructure, DB2 for z/OS, with new technologies in order to maximize your investment and drive new value for your customers."

Located at IBM's Silicon Valley Laboratory, Tom is the director of IBM's premiere relational database management system. His responsibilities include Architecture, Development, Service, and Customer Support for DB2. He leads development labs in the United States, Germany, and China. Tom works closely with IBM's largest clients to ensure that DB2 for z/OS continues as the leading solution for modern applications, encompassing OLTP to mobile to analytics. At the same time he continues an uncompromising focus on meeting the needs of the most demanding operational environments on Earth, through DB2's industry-leading performance, availability, scaling, and security capabilities.

IBM DB2 for z/OS: The Database for Gaining a Competitive Advantage!

Shantan Kethireddy

Jane Man

Surekha Parekh

Pallavi Priyadarshini

Maryela Weihrauch

MC Press Online, LLC
Boise, ID 83703 USA

IBM DB2 for z/OS: The Database for Gaining a Competitive Advantage!
*Shantan Kethireddy, Jane Man, Surekha Parekh, Pallavi Priyadarshini, and
Maryela Weihrauch*

First Edition
First Printing—October 2015

The following terms are trademarks or registered trademarks of International Business
Machines Corporation in the United States, other countries, or both: IBM, CICS, Cognos,
DB2, Guardium, IBM MobileFirst, PureData, RACF, SPSS, System z, WebSphere, z
Systems, zEnterprise, and z/OS. Netezza® is a registered trademark of IBM International
Group B.V., an IBM Company. A current list of IBM trademarks is available on the Web
at *http://www.ibm.com/legal/copytrade.shtml.*

Java and all Java-based trademarks and logos are trademarks or registered trademarks of
Oracle and/or its affiliates. Apache, Hadoop, and Spark are trademarks of The Apache
Software Foundation. Linux is a registered trademark of Linus Torvalds in the United
States, other countries, or both. Other company, product, or service names may be
trademarks or service marks of others.

Every attempt has been made to provide correct information. However, the publisher and
the authors do not guarantee the accuracy of the book and do not assume responsibility
for information included in or omitted from it.

This document is current as of the initial date of publication and may be changed by IBM
at any time. Not all offerings are available in every country in which IBM operates. The
performance data and client examples cited are presented for illustrative purposes only.
Actual performance results may vary depending on specific configurations and operating
conditions.

It is the user's responsibility to evaluate and verify the operation of any other products or
programs with IBM products and programs.

THE INFORMATION IN THIS DOCUMENT IS PROVIDED "AS IS" WITHOUT
ANY WARRANTY, EXPRESS OR IMPLIED, INCLUDING WITHOUT ANY
WARRANTIES OF MERCHANTABILITY, FITNESS FOR A PARTICULAR
PURPOSE AND ANY WARRANTY OR CONDITION OF NON-INFRINGEMENT.

IBM products are warranted according to the terms and conditions of the agreements under
which they are provided. Statements regarding IBM's future direction and intent are subject
to change or withdrawal without notice, and represent goals and objectives only.

MC Press Online, LLC
Corporate Offices: 3695 W. Quail Heights Court, Boise, ID 83703-3861 USA
Sales and Customer Service: (208) 629-7275 ext. 500; service@mcpressonline.com
Permissions and Bulk/Special Orders: mcbooks@mcpressonline.com
www.mcpressonline.com • www.mc-store.com

ISBN: 978-1-58347-437-2   WB201510

About the Authors

Shantan Kethireddy (*shantank@us.ibm.com*) is an IBM Master Inventor and a technical sales specialist for Information Management solutions on z Systems products. In this role, he is responsible for leading consultative business value validation engagements for big data and analytics. He holds a Masters in Computer Engineering and Electrical Engineering from the University of Iowa and possesses two dozen patents, primarily focused on data-centric technologies.

"New technologies are challenging the traditional perceptions that MPP systems are less expensive for executing CPU-intensive data queries. Today, z Systems technologies have the ability to cost-effectively execute those queries while simultaneously reducing your risk of a data breach and your IT TCO. To learn more about these technologies and how they've worked for large enterprises, please read "Could Your Analytics Strategy Cost Your Business $100M?" page 9.

Jane Man (*janeman@us.ibm.com*) is a Senior Software Engineer in the DB2 for z/OS development team, and has worked on various features of DB2 for z/OS. In addition to her development work, Jane is the enablement focal point and is involved in many enablement activities, such as creating sample applications, demos, and Hands-on Labs, and presenting in conferences and bootcamps.

Before joining DB2 for z/OS, Jane was a developer on the IBM Content Manager team. Jane is an IBM Certified System Administrator for WebSphere Application Server; IBM Certified Database Administrator for DB2 Universal Database for z/OS, Linux, UNIX and Windows; IBM Certified Solution Designer for DB2 Content Manager; IBM Certified Deployment Profession for Tivoli Storage Manager; and IBM Certified Application Developer for the DB2 Universal Database Family.

"I strongly encourage any customer planning a migration to DB2 11, or even already executing a project to migrate to DB2 11, to read this book, as it will help the respective installation migrate faster and safely to the new release."

Surekha Parekh (*surekhaparekh@uk.ibm.com*) is IBM's WW Marketing Portfolio Director, DB2 for z/OS. She has more than 25 years' experience in B2B Market Management across a broad range of IT products and solutions with proven results. Surekha currently leads the Marketing for DB2 for z/OS globally and is responsible for market strategy, planning, and execution of tactics in IBM.

A successful campaign and brand manager, Surekha has led several IBM global campaigns, including the 30th Anniversary of DB2. She is customer-focused and understands the importance of Customer Relationship Management. Surekha also leads the Social Media Strategy for Information Management on System z. and has built several loyal social media communities for IBM on LinkedIn, Twitter, Google+, and Facebook, with over 10,000 members. Surekha also developed "The World of DB2" community (*www.worldofdb2.com*), a dedicated DB2 online community with over 3,000 members.

Based in Warwick, United Kingdom, Surekha is a passionate marketer and a member of Chartered Marketers. She represents IBM on the International DB2 User Group (IDUG) committee and is currently the IDUG Marketing Chair.

"We hope you enjoy this book. It is segmented into five areas, and each paper is focused on one of these game-changing technologies —Cloud, Analytics, and Mobile—which are creating a knowledge revolution and helping companies to transform the way they do business today. Data is the newest natural resource for enterprises, and the market winners will be the organizations that leverage their existing investment to innovate and gain a deeper business insight without impacting security and trust. Find out why DB2 for z/OS is still the #1 Trusted Data Server for most Fortune 100® companies, and learn how to exploit your data to gain a competitive edge."

Pallavi Priyadarshini (*pallavipr@in.ibm.com*) is the Architect and Product Manager of DB2 Connect portfolio and works out of India Software Labs. Pallavi has over 14 years of experience in product development and enjoys working with the latest technologies in Cloud and Analytics. She has designed and developed key features in the DB2 z/OS server in Silicon Valley Labs. She has also developed Web-based and security applications as part of two Silicon Valley startups. Pallavi regularly delivers best-practices presentations at conferences and is the technical advocate for global enterprise accounts.

Pallavi also has authored patents and publications in data-centric solutions. She completed her Masters in Computer Science from San Jose State University, California, and Bachelors in Computer Science from Nanyang Technological University, Singapore.

"The technology landscape is undergoing a revolution, with every company investing in Cloud, Mobile, and Advanced Analytics for Big Data. These three technology pillars promise to be game-changers for businesses—as they will determine the ability of businesses to respond to the market fast and offer differentiated value to their customers. DB2 for z/OS is delivering innovations in these areas—and is constantly building upon its track record of unbeaten quality of service for mission-critical enterprise data. Read this book to find out how integration of DB2 for z/OS with the latest technologies will help you make your enterprise data ready for the next generation of applications."

Maryela Weihrauch (*weihrau@us.ibm.com*) is an IBM Distinguished Engineer with DB2 for z/OS Development. She has been working with customers around the world to design their DB2 systems and applications for optimum performance and availability. Currently, she drives the Business Analytic strategy with DB2 for z/OS. Maryela frequently shares her experience at conferences.

Contents

About the Authors v

Introduction *by Surekha Parekh* xiii

DB2 for z/OS and Cloud Computing
  by Surekha Parekh and Maryela Weihrauch 1

Highlights 1

Introduction
  What Is Cloud Computing, and What Is Driving This Market Trend? 1

IBM Cloud Computing Is Designed for Business 2

  What Is Data as a Service, and What Are the Drivers? 2

DB2 for z/OS 2

Cloud Configurations 4

DB2 for z/OS Cloud Provisioning 4

Cloud Infrastructure in IBM z Systems 4

IBM z/OS Management Facility 5

DB2 and z/OS Management Facility 6

Additional Benefits and Features 6

Why IBM? 7

For More Information 7

  Notes 7

**Could Your Analytics Strategy Cost Your Business $100M? Learn
How New Technologies Can Help Protect Your Analytics, Data, and
Your Bottom Line**
  by Shantan Kethireddy 9

Introduction: Your Data Is Not Safe 9

The Data Origination Challenge 10

System Costs 11

System Cost Solutions 13

Data Security 15

Example Healthcare Company Analysis 16

Data Security Solutions 17

System Performance 18

System Performance Solutions..19
Data Archiving 19
Data Archiving Solutions 20
Performance, Security, and Savings..21
How IBM Can Help Your Bottom Line...21
For More Information..22
  Notes 23

Predictive Analytics Using IBM SPSS Modeler in DB2 for z/OS
  by Jane Man, Lei Tian, and Liang Wang....................................25
Introduction 25
  Why DB2 for z/OS Customers May Want to Use SPSS and
    the Business Value...25
Setup and Configuration..26
Building a Simple Model Using Data Stored in DB2 for z/OS..................27
  Step 1: Configure the ODBC DSN. 27
  Step 2: Build a simple model using data from DB2 for z/OS. 30
Scoring Inside DB2 for z/OS via Modeler UDF
  (Server Scoring Adapter) 38
Scoring Inside DB2 for z/OS via SQL Pushback 41
Publishing the Model into DB2 for z/OS 44
Creating an SQL Statement to Perform In-Database Real-time Scoring 48
Summary 51
Acknowledgments...51
Appendix: Load/Insert Data into DB2 for z/OS.......................................52
Resources 54

Maximizing Mobile Initiatives with IBM DB2 for z/OS
  by Surekha Parekh and Mark Simmonds 55
Introduction 55
The Need for Banks to Become Customer Centric 55
The Mobile Tipping Point...57
Mobile Redefines the Business and Responsibilities 58

Banking Your Business on a Mobile Strategy—
the DB2 for z/OS Advantage 58

Case study: Reducing costs and accelerating time to value with
analytics and mobile on the mainframe 59

The Need for Speed, Data Currency, and Security..................................... 60

Under the Hood of a Secure and Fraud-Resistant Mobile Transaction 61

Reuse Services and Data to Build Portable Mobile Apps 63

Reducing the Complexity of Multiple Mobile Platform Support.................. 63

IBM z Systems—Designed for the Mobile Era.. 65

Case study: Growing the business with a secure
multi-channel business.. 66

Conclusion.. 67

For More Information... 67

Notes 68

DB2 for z/OS and Spark Integration

DB2 and Spark—the Perfect Partner for Big Data

by Pallavi Priyadarshini 69

Introduction: What Is Spark? 69

IBM and Apache Spark: The Start of Something Big in Data
and Design... 69

Apache Spark and DB2 for z/OS 69

Blog 1: Using Spark's Interactive Scala Shell for Accessing DB2 Data
Using JDBC Driver and Spark's New DataFrames API............................. 72

Blog 2: Accessing DB2 Data from Spark via Standalone Scala/
Java Programs in Eclipse 77

Blog 3: Simplify Joining DB2 Data and JSON Data with Spark 88

Blog 4: Persisting Spark DataFrames into DB2 92

Conclusion.. 95

Introduction: The Changing World of Data

by Surekha Parekh

Cloud, Big Data, Analytics, and Mobile are changing the landscape for enterprise customers, and this change is driving greater need than ever for Security. The use of data and devices is exploding right before our eyes. This paradigm shift presents unique opportunities and challenges for enterprise companies wanting to leverage data and analytics to differentiate and gain a competitive advantage.

Few organizations can keep pace with the appetite for data. As business professionals recognize the revenue potential from analyzing and acting on insight, demand for data escalates. But systems and budgets can't keep up with the increased demand, the complexity of all the types of data, and the need to act fast. Current IT infrastructures just aren't sustainable. Top-performing organizations confront this reality by balancing the costs, risks, and benefits of sustaining their existing architecture while adopting new technologies and platforms.

Why DB2 for z/OS?

To fully capitalize on their data for competitive advantage, enterprises must have the right database infrastructure in place. DB2 for z/OS is well equipped to furnish enterprise customers the insights that will drive revenue, improve responsiveness, and help them stay ahead of the competition. The upcoming next release of DB2 for z/OS—DB2 12—scheduled for availability in 2016, is expected to further evolve the platform's analytics capabilities.

On October 6, 2015, IBM announced DB2 12 for z/OS Early Support Program; IBM will be making DB2 12 available to select customers starting March 4, 2016. You could think of this as a "beta," although it is much more, in our opinion.

What will DB2 12 deliver? It's way too early to start going into any detail; so much can happen between now and when the product is actually delivered. However, what we can tell you is that DB2 12 is built on the proven, trusted availability, security, and scalability of DB2 11 for z/OS and the IBM z Systems platform—the gold standard in the industry. DB2 12 will give you the capabilities required to meet the business demands of the future and will help enterprises exploit data and information and gain knowledge and wisdom.

DB2 12 delivers innovations in these key areas—and much more:

- Scale and speed for the next era of mobile applications and interconnected devices (Internet of Things, or IoT)
- Speedy in-memory database performance for innovation
- Next-generation application development support for CAMS (Cloud, Analytics, Mobile, and Security) and deeper insights
- Easy access to your enterprise systems of record

DB2 for z/OS Is Ready for Cloud, Analytics, Mobile, and Spark

This book is divided into five segments, related to Cloud, Analytics, Mobile, and Spark:

1. DB2 for z/OS and Cloud Computing
2. Could Your Analytics Strategy Cost Your Business $100M? Learn How New Technologies Can Help Protect Your Analytics, Data, and Your Bottom Line
3. Predictive Analytics Using IBM SPSS Modeler in DB2 for z/OS
4. Maximizing Mobile Initiatives with IBM DB2 for z/OS
5. DB2 for z/OS and Spark Integration

1. DB2 for z/OS and Cloud Computing

Most people probably realize that data is extremely valuable. However, what they may not realize is that together, data and cloud help address key business challenges that clients face when they apply data and analytics to their business. As data shifts rapidly to the cloud, enterprises are looking to both mine those data sources and perform analytics on them. This trend is changing the face of the market, creating opportunities for new buyers—from business analysts to developers.

IBM DB2 for z/OS includes a cloud solution that offers organizations the opportunity to remove expensive hardware and move to a responsive, virtual environment. With DB2 for z/OS on the cloud, you can reduce cost and complexity in your IT infrastructure, simplify compliance, and get the most out of your core asset—your data, without impacting security. In this section, you'll learn how by moving to the cloud, you can transform and adapt while limiting risk and cost to achieve agility and efficiency by standardizing best practices.

2. Could Your Analytics Strategy Cost Your Business $100M? Learn How New Technologies Can Help Protect Your Analytics, Data, and Your Bottom Line

Technology trends and forces such as cloud, mobile, and big data can represent big opportunities to bring analytic insight to the enterprise. They can also represent big risks if proper data security and governance controls are not in place. In 2015, one of the largest health benefits companies in the United States reported that its systems were the target of a massive data breach. This exposed millions of records containing sensitive consumer information, such as Social Security numbers, medical IDs, and income information. Various sources, including The Insurance Insider, suggest that this company's $100 million cyber-insurance policy would be depleted by the costs of notifying consumers of the breach and providing credit monitoring services—and that doesn't consider other significant costs associated with a breach such as lost business, regulatory fines, and lawsuits.

Data is now so important that it is has a value on the balance sheet. Cyber criminals know this. Without exception, every industry has been under attack and suffered data breaches: healthcare, government, banking, insurance, retail, and telecommunications. Once a company has been breached, hackers focus on other companies in that same industry to exploit similar vulnerabilities. In 2015 the average cost of a data breach was $3.79 million, causing long term damage to the brand, loss of faith and customer churn.

As you think about the impacts of this and other data security breaches occurring at organizations worldwide, consider this question: how exposed is your business to a similar type of breach? To answer this question, you must first ask, "Where does the data that feeds our analytics processes originate?" Read this paper to gain a deeper insight.

3. Predictive Analytics Using IBM SPSS Modeler in DB2 for z/OS

This section focuses on predictive analytics using IBM SPSS Modeler and data stored in IBM DB2 for z/OS. We illustrate how to use the Modeler Workbench to create predictive models with in-database mining, SQL pushback, and user-defined function scoring. You will walk through the steps for integrating real-time scoring for DB2 for z/OS into an OLTP application. Then, you'll learn what needs to be done in the DB2 server and the information an application developer needs to know to create an enterprise solution for in-database transactional scoring and batch scoring.

4. Maximizing Mobile Initiatives with IBM DB2 for z/OS

Mobile is becoming the primary mode of transaction and delivery for critical business insight. Mobile provides clients with the means to securely improve visibility and control, connect with customers in context, and create new value at the moment of awareness. 50.3 percent of e-commerce website traffic comes through a mobile device (source: Shopify), and 60 percent of global mobile consumers use their mobile device as their primary or exclusive Internet source (source: Internet Retailer). This section discusses how and why mobile computing solutions built around IBM® z Systems™ and IBM DB2® for z/OS® can help banks deliver on business challenges around reducing costs, improving awareness of security needs, understanding customers, and increasing market share.

5. DB2 for z/OS and Spark Integration

Apache® Spark™ is an open source cluster computing framework with in-memory processing to speed analytic applications up to 100 times faster compared to technologies on the market today. Developed in the AMPLab at University of California, Berkeley, Apache Spark can help reduce data interaction complexity, increase processing speed, and enhance mission-critical applications with deep intelligence. Highly versatile in many environments, Apache Spark is known for its ease of use in creating algorithms that harness insight from complex data.

Spark was elevated to a top-level Apache Project in 2014 and continues to expand today. IBM is committing to the Apache Spark project with investments in design-led innovation and broad-scale education programs to promote open source innovation and accelerate intelligence into every application. Since DB2 is the preferred system of record for structured data, an integration of Spark with DB2 is an obvious next step in the evolution of Big Data. Customers often have a need to perform analytics on not just pure DB2 data, but aggregate DB2 data with other data sources to derive additional business insights. In this section, you'll learn how to integrate Spark with DB2 for z/OS data.

We hope you enjoy this book.

Surekha Parekh, WW Marketing Program Director
IBM Corporation Ltd.

DB2 for z/OS and Cloud Computing

by Surekha Parekh and Maryela Weihrauch

Highlights

- Highly virtualized server that supports mixed workloads
- Self-serving capabilities in private, membership or hybrid cloud environments
- Divisional support of responsibilities
- Customized implementations to suit your business
- Platform foundation services for cloud use cases

Introduction

What Is Cloud Computing, and What Is Driving This Market Trend?

Cloud computing is a platform that allows on-demand, pay-for-use access to applications or computing resources, as services, from the Internet. The era of cloud computing is a paradigm shift that is occurring as the result of severe market competition and a dramatically changing business environment. Firms are being prompted to adopt various state-of-the-art information solutions to improve their business operations. The drivers for implementing cloud computing services are:

- Improve speed of business
- Reduce costs
- Improve customer communications
- Facilitate mobilization
- Manage the increase in the variety, velocity and type of data

IBM Cloud Computing Is Designed for Business

Many industry-leading companies use IBM cloud computing.

Why? With the IBM cloud, you can unlock more value in your business and in the technology you already have. The cloud can integrate enterprise-grade services and help speed up the way you innovate.

What Is Data as a Service, and What Are the Drivers?

According to the analyst firm Ovum, data as a service (DaaS) is a natural and logical evolution of the as-a-service model.[1] As the volume, variety, and complexity of data continue to increase, the skills that are necessary to master them become proportionally scarcer. Transferring the burden of data sourcing and management, and allowing users to focus on finding value in its use, require little endorsement for many organizations.

DaaS for business empowers businesses to use data as a standalone asset and to connect with partner data to make smarter decisions. IBM® DB2® for z/OS® DaaS is a service in the IBM cloud that is designed to offer variety, scale, and connectivity. It includes cross-channel, cross-device, and known and anonymous data without compromising reliability, availability and security.

DB2 for z/OS

Many of the world's top banks, retailers, and insurance providers store mission-critical operational data in IBM z Systems™ and DB2 for z/OS. DB2 for z/OS and z Systems are designed to handle rapidly changing, diverse, and unpredictable workloads while maximizing resource utilization and investment. Simply put, DB2 for z/OS is among the most scalable, reliable, and cost-effective data servers available.

The mainframe was originally designed to handle a complete range of applications, from small to large, both commercial and scientific. Virtualization of hardware and efficiency of operation have now become significant areas of impact in technology today.

IBM DB2 for z/OS includes a cloud solution that offers organizations the opportunity to remove expensive hardware and move to a responsive, virtual environment (Figure 1).

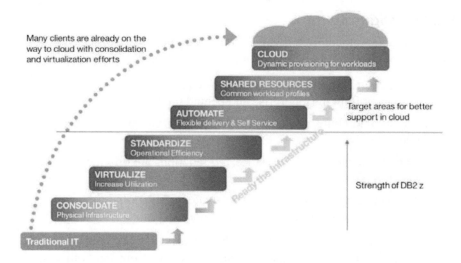

Figure 1: Movement from traditional DB2 for z/OS environments to the cloud

With DB2 for z/OS on the cloud, you can reduce cost and complexity in your IT infrastructure, simplify compliance, and get the most out of your core asset — your data, without impacting security. By moving to the cloud, you can transform and adapt while limiting risk and cost to achieve agility and efficiency by standardizing best practices.

Many enterprise companies consolidate their IT infrastructure, operating in a service-provider model for their business units. They already implemented methods to automate the delivery of IT solutions, mostly driven by the need to reduce the cost of the IT infrastructure.

IBM z Systems and the IBM products that run on these systems—including DB2 for z/OS—use cloud support. This support provides functionality for dynamic provisioning of IT solutions to potentially replace individual approaches and shift to a self-service mode of operation.

IBM DB2 for z/OS experts have prioritized the seamless transition of the solution to a cloud environment. In response to the growing demand for organizations to move to the cloud, IBM has placed essential focus on the technical support that is required to effect a successful transition.

Although the technical hurdles must be cleared with efficiency and proficiency, a successful transition to the cloud has another essential requirement. That is, use deployment on the cloud as a way to improve the overall consumability of DB2 for z/OS for clients, from usability to functionality to access to performance.

Cloud Configurations

Discussions about cloud often revolve around a public virtual space. Looking closer, other types of cloud configurations are possible:

- **The private cloud**—IT capabilities are provided as a service, over an intranet, within the enterprise and behind the firewall.
- **The hybrid cloud**—Internal and external service delivery methods are integrated.
- **The public cloud**—IT activities and functions are provided as a service over the Internet.

Whether your organization chooses a private, public or hybrid cloud, management and hosting options still remain open.

Selecting a managed private cloud or hosted private cloud depends on your database management strategy and budgetary concerns. Consider both areas when making the best choice for your company.

Enhancements in DB2 for z/OS in support of cloud use cases focus on requirements from enterprises that support private and hybrid cloud configurations.

DB2 for z/OS Cloud Provisioning

DB2 can be provisioned as a software stack, and variations can be accommodated upon installation. The DB2 environment scope can include:

- A DB2 system
- Migration to a new version of a DB2 system
- A database in an existing DB2 system
- Access to an existing database in an existing DB2 system
- A copy of an existing database

Cloud Infrastructure in IBM z Systems

The appropriate cloud infrastructure should be designed to support the division of responsibilities and the ability to customize implementation. The functionality that is needed in support of the public cloud is different from the functionality that is needed in support of a private or hybrid cloud.

Enterprises often report that they need the speed of self-service, but that they would not compromise operational efficiency. Essentially, they are accustomed to a highly customized environment.

Additionally, IBM z Systems environments are highly virtualized and shared. Many subject matter experts are involved in cloud service provisioning use cases to cover different aspects of system management, such as storage, networking, and security.

The infrastructure for cloud use cases should be designed to seamlessly incorporate the separation of responsibilities.

IBM z/OS Management Facility

IBM z/OS Management Facility helps to improve the repeatability of tasks and improve efficiencies while saving time and workforce expenditures. z/OS Management Facility is also designed to use role-based assignments, creating clear workforce tasks while minimizing questions about who should perform which task.

z/OS Management Facility delivers the following features:

- Workflow capability that is designed to help improve the ability to repeat tasks:
    - Sequences the flow of tasks to manage the configuration of the system.
    - Uses role-based assignments and issues notifications to alert users about their next steps in the process.
    - Helps users simplify work through guided steps, assign responsibilities, and track progress, all by using the workflows task.
- A guided flow through the steps to accomplish a task:
    - XML metadata file that contains steps and details
    - Wizards to update and submit jobs and to execute shell scripts and REXX execs
    - Step features:
        - Manual or automated in a wizard
        - Dependency on other steps
        - Various stages until completion
        - Option to skip or override steps
    - History of all activities in the workflow task

DB2 and z/OS Management Facility

To help you understand how z/OS Management Facility works with DB2 for z/OS, assume that an application needs a function that is provided in the latest version of DB2.

As a step of the application deployment, you need to migrate the existing DB2 system to that new version. Traditionally, this approach involves running many migration steps. For some of these steps, you must manually check or run them, which is a long and involved process.

Now, the migration steps can be expressed in customized z/OS Management Facility workflows, assigned to the responsible user ID and run automatically. Default z/OS Management Facility workflow artifacts for common DB2 provisioning use cases are introduced in DB2 11. You can customize them (for example: remove steps, add steps, or change steps) to reflect the specific configuration of a DB2 system or group of systems that support similar workload characteristics.

Additional Benefits and Features

A redeployment of your existing DB2 for z/OS environment to the cloud or another space is a significant transition. IBM is prepared and equipped to help your organization undergo such an undertaking.

Beyond the redeployment, DB2 for z/OS provides additional features and benefits:

- Improved Java data access performance without changing code
- Custom-developed, framework-based or packaged application
- A bind tool
- Static SQL execution value to existing DB2 for z/OS applications
- More predictable and stable response times
- Limits on user access to tables by granting execute privileges on query packages
- Aid for forecasting accuracy and capacity planning
- Decreased CPU cycles to increase overall capability
- A choice between dynamic or static execution at deployment time

Why IBM?

IBM DB2 for z/OS teams have a long history, experience, and technical expertise in working with physical and virtual DB2 for z/OS deployments, including transitions to public, private, or hybrid cloud environments. IBM is committed to supporting the entire spectrum of DB2 for z/OS deployments and transitions, and IBM's cloud-focused strategies are custom-implemented for organizations that are looking to make that transition.

For More Information

For more information about using IBM DB2 for z/OS in the cloud, see the following websites:

- IBM DB2 for z/OS: *ibm.com/software/data/db2/zos/family*
- IBM z/OS Management Facility: *ibm.com/systems/z/os/ zos/features/zosmf*
- IBM cloud computing: *ibm.com/cloud-computing/us/en*

Notes

1. Tom Pringle, "Data-as-a-service: the Next Step in the As-a-service Journey," Ovum, 18 July 2014: *www.ovum.com/research/data-as-a-service-the- next-step-in-the-as-a-service-journey*.

Could Your Analytics Strategy Cost Your Business $100M? Learn How New Technologies Can Help Protect Your Analytics, Data, and Your Bottom Line

by Shantan Kethireddy

Introduction

Your Data Is Not Safe

Technology trends and forces, including cloud, mobile and big data, can create large opportunities for your enterprise to exploit analytic insights. But the same things that enable these opportunities can skyrocket your risks if proper data security and governance controls are not in place.

As an example, in 2015 one of the largest health benefits companies in the United States reported that its systems were the target of a massive data breach. This breach exposed millions of records containing sensitive consumer information such as social security numbers, medical IDs and income information.

Various sources, including The Insurance Insider, suggest that this company's USD 100 million cyber-insurance policy would be depleted by the costs of notifying consumers of the breach and providing credit-monitoring services. And that policy payout doesn't consider other significant costs associated with a breach such as lost business, regulatory fines and lawsuits.

Cyber criminals now know the same thing every industry analyst knows—data is so important it has a value on the balance sheet. For that reason, every single industry has been attacked by hackers and experienced data breaches, including healthcare, government, banking, insurance, retail and telecommunications. Furthermore, once one company has been breached, hackers focus on other companies in that same industry hoping to exploit similar vulnerabilities.

So while this incident is one of the higher-cost examples, with a worldwide average data breach cost of USD 3.79 million[1], coupled with the long-term brand damage, loss of faith and customer churn, consider this question: how exposed is your business to a similar type of breach? To answer this question, you must first ask, "Where does the data that feeds our analytics processes originate?"

The Data Origination Challenge

For many enterprise clients, the answer to the data origination question is that the data comes from an IBM® z Systems™ mainframe. That is because organizations often run their mission-critical applications on z Systems to take advantage of its industry-leading service qualities such as availability, reliability, and Evaluation Assurance Level (EAL) 5+ security.

Unfortunately, a large percentage of these organizations then weaken that security by replicating or transferring sensitive data off their IBM z Systems mainframe. They do this for a variety of reasons, including realizing perceived cost savings, conducting analysis on massively parallel processing (MPP) systems, combining with data from external sources, or satisfying end-user technology preferences.

Whether it be quick, short online transaction processing (OLTP), analytical operational queries, or highly concurrent, lighter-weight workloads, the IBM DB2® for z/OS® database has historically handled mixed workloads well. However, to run CPU-intensive queries that involve processing large amounts of data in parallel, including analytics that group, sort, and aggregate, organizations using DB2 for z/OS would typically employ one of the following options:

- Use data administration (indexing, partitioning, materialized query table) to address each individual query, which can be labor intensive.
- Purchase additional hardware resources, which can be cost prohibitive.
- Use a resource limit facility (RLF) or similar product to prevent these queries from consuming too many resources, which can shunt a potentially valuable or necessary workload.
- Extract data to disparate systems capable of performing the CPU-intensive parallel processing, which is the most common approach because it appears to be less costly.

The reality is that replicating or extracting data off z System mainframes has led to a proliferation of data repositories containing personally identifiable information and silos of disparate people, processes, and infrastructure (PPI). Figure 1 illustrates this graphically.

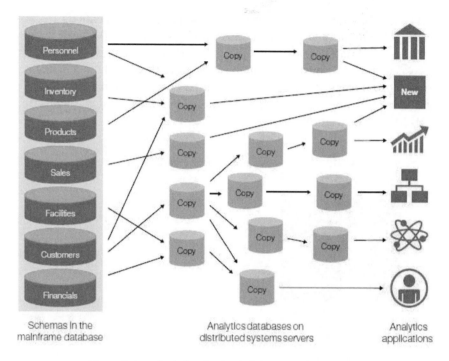

Figure 1: A replicated and extracted data repository structure

For larger organizations, this structure can occur repeatedly. That is because each line of business (LOB) often has its own PPI that is typically managed and billed through chargeback. Each LOB then uses its own data repository, sourced from a z Systems platform, choosing PPI because it is available and familiar rather than the perceived challenge of employing the data from the source.

While often the default choice, deploying replicated and extracted data repositories can increase your organization's risk exposure across the spectrum. For this discussion, we'll focus on the four most crucial risk areas: system costs, data security, system performance, and data archiving.

System Costs

Some organizations view reducing data breach liability as cost avoidance. Since IT architecture decisions are often made based on the best hard dollar cost solution, they may not account for cost avoidance best practices that include limiting the data breach threat. This mindset, along with the pervasive view that DB2 for z/OS is primarily useful for OLTP workloads, has contributed to the growth of disparate data repositories for analytics workloads.

New DB2 for z/OS technologies targeted at analytics applications are challenging this traditional view and transforming the hard dollar cost comparisons. As Figure 2 illustrates, comparisons now often reveal the hard dollar costs to extract, transfer, and load (ETL) or replicate data to a disparate environment for analysis exceeds the hard dollar cost to keep the data on z Systems and apply new technologies such as IBM DB2 Analytics Accelerator or IBM DB2 Value Unit Edition.

Figure 2: Potential cost savings compared to replicating 200 GB of data per day per database environment.[2]

While the USD 333,479 expense is substantial, it is just one instance. A typical LOB organization will have multiple instances of each data repository for unit test, system test, user acceptance test, and production. Consequently, the costs—and the savings—are generally multiplied by a factor of four.

In this example, that means the traditional ETL approach costs almost USD 1 million more than executing analytics on the z Systems mainframe. For an enterprise with multiple LOBs, you can see how the extra annual costs for data extraction or replication can quickly add up to millions of dollars.

If you closely examine the cost components, you can see how this happens. In addition to costs usually accounted for in a hard dollar cost comparison, the true costs should account for all actual expenditures, including additional managed infrastructure costs as well as additional IT administration costs.

For example, once data is replicated to a disparate environment, there are real managed infrastructure costs associated with using, administering, and maintaining that environment. Many organizations rely on various internal or outsourced infrastructure teams to manage these environments and then bill the client through internal chargeback.

The IT administration costs come from development efforts to make the DB2 for z/OS source data usable and consumable. While typically not included in chargeback or actual data movement costs, these jobs have real costs associated with them. Examples of these costs include building ETL flows to extract the data from DB2 for z/OS; denormalizing the data, which includes combining data from different platforms; and performing data transformations, adding surrogate keys and table lookups as well as loading the data into the remote data store.

Often, the cost of building and maintaining these flows, along with adjusting for detected changes, represents the largest ongoing and growing financial liability for the IT organization. As more end users are supported and data volumes grow, the cost to extract, transform, load, and render that data explodes.

In addition, the change detection, change management, and change test and deployment activities become very challenging and therefore costly. Fortunately, the IBM Eagle Team has developed total cost of ownership (TCO) analysis tools that incorporate these expenditures into TCO analyses; additional details can obtained by emailing *eagletco@us.ibm.com.*

System Cost Solutions

Much of the data sprawl off z System mainframes was triggered by the traditional belief that z Systems were not the most cost-effective option for handling CPU-intensive analytic workloads, and that PPIs allowed for more efficient integration of data from external sources. New technologies are challenging this belief in a variety of ways.

For example, software costs can be drastically reduced using specialty engines such as z System Integrated Information Processors (zIIPs), z System Application Assist Processors (zAAPs), and Integrated Facilities for Linux (IFLs). In addition, z System CPUs typically exhibit 100 percent utilization in a mixed-workload environment. Most importantly, three IBM offerings can dramatically impact the economics of keeping source data in DB2 for z/OS:

- DB2 Analytics Accelerator
- DB2 Value Unit Edition
- z System Collocated Application Pricing (zCAP)

The IBM DB2 Analytics Accelerator for z/OS is a high-performance appliance for DB2 for z/OS. It deeply integrates the IBM z Systems infrastructure with IBM PureData® Systems for Analytics, which is powered by IBM Netezza® technology.

With the DB2 Analytics Accelerator, DB2 for z/OS can offload data-intensive and complex static and dynamic DB2 for z/OS queries, such as data warehousing, business intelligence, and analytic workloads, transparently to the application. The DB2 Analytics Accelerator then executes these queries significantly faster than previously possible—all while avoiding CPU utilization by DB2 for z/OS.

The DB2 Analytics Accelerator price-performance curve also opens unprecedented opportunities for organizations to use data on their z Systems. It allows users to run workloads that historically were offloaded from z Systems, or run queries that were governed or shunted in DB2 for z/OS, such as ad hoc queries whose performance characteristics are typically unknown at runtime. And IT administrators can allow DB2 for z/OS to choose where to run these queries, or they can force these queries to the DB2 Analytics Accelerator to prevent additional DB2 for z/OS consumption.

While the DB2 Analytics Accelerator is a separate piece of hardware, it is a logical extension of DB2 for z/OS because DB2 for z/OS manages and regulates all access to the DB2 Analytics Accelerator. This means DB2 for z/OS will continue to handle those workloads that make sense to run in DB2 for z/OS, like OLTP queries and operational analytics, and it will reroute those queries that best fit an MPP technology to the DB2 Analytics Accelerator.

Beyond the pure analysis capabilities, the DB2 Analytics Accelerator also includes the ability to perform in-database transformations and multi-step processing using Accelerator-only tables. And with technologies like the IBM DB2 Analytics Accelerator Loader for z/OS, users can quickly load data from DB2 for z/OS along with non-DB2 and non-mainframe data directly into the DB2 Analytics Accelerator without interrupting access to production objects. This can reduce the need to denormalize the data, historically a major reason for offloading z System data.

While the DB2 Analytics Accelerator adds a cost-effective, secure solution for CPU-intensive workloads, IBM also offers a DB2 for z/OS licensing option called DB2 Value Unit Edition (DB2 VUE). With DB2 VUE, clients can deploy

DB2 for z/OS using a one-time charge (OTC) model as opposed to the traditional monthly licensing charge (MLC) model.

Taking advantage of the OTC approach helps shift the cost of qualifying new workloads from an operating expense (OPEX) to a capital expense (CAPEX). This allows you to consolidate new workloads back to DB2 for z/OS, and manage those workloads as they grow to meet the demands of end users—all without increasing MLC costs.

The third offering that influences the costs of executing data analytics is z System Collocated Application Pricing (zCAP). zCAP can improve the cost of deploying new z/OS applications by allowing new applications to be deployed in existing logical partitions (LPARs) but priced as if they were running in dedicated LPARs. More information is available at *https://ibm.biz/BdXQe9*.

This enhancement to sub-capacity reporting removes up to 100 percent of the new application's general-purpose processor time from the machine utilization values reported for other middleware, and up to 50 percent for z/OS.[3] The result is you only pay for the new application's direct usage of the IBM middleware that manages the processing of the new application—such as CICS, IBM WebSphere® Application Server, IMS, and DB2 for z/OS—while mitigating the impact on the million service units (MSU) reported for other programs running in the same partition.

Data Security

As the health benefits company data breach illustrates, the practice of extracting or replicating data to disparate PPI systems poses serious security concerns. And each PPI instance substantially increases your potential liability from a data breach.

By definition, creating more copies of sensitive information increases the risks of a data breach. This is because each LOB may have its own data encryption policies, its own policies on credential governance, its own policies on disseminating analyzed data, and its own level of policy enforcement of these policies. Perhaps more important, each copy of that data has its own set of interfaces for accessing that data.

So, typically there will be a separate set of authentication mechanisms for each data store. For example, DB2 for z/OS data is protected via IBM RACF® security. But a copy of that data in a distributed database management system (DBMS) will typically be protected using a separate Lightweight Directory Access Protocol (LDAP) server that may be combined with DBMS credentials. Each copy then presents an additional potential entry point for a hacker.

Example Healthcare Company Analysis

As an example, let's use findings from the Ponemon Institute's report, "2014 Cost of Data Breach Study: Global Analysis," to illustrate the cost of a 10,000-record data breach risk to a healthcare company.

The per capita data breach cost = USD 359 per record, from Figure 3. The probability of a data breach per year: 22.2 ÷ 2 = 11.1 percent per year, from Figure 4. At 2 KB per record, data breach costs are USD 0.18 per byte, or USD 180,000 per MB. For each 10,000 records, or 20 MB, the average data breach cost is 20 MB × USD 180,000 per MB × 11.1 percent probability per year = USD 400,000 per year.

For a company supporting 10 distributed databases that have been extracted or replicated from a DB2 for z/OS system, this can equate to an estimated increased annual cost of USD 4.0 million due to security risks.

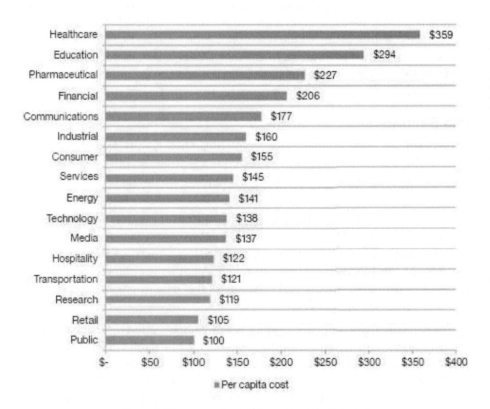

Figure 3: The per capita data breach cost by industry[4]

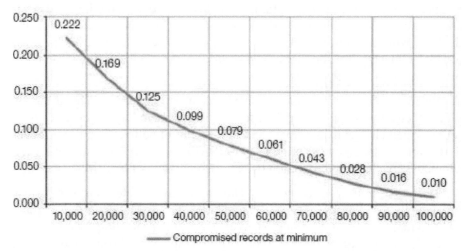

Compromised records at minimum

Figure 4: The probability of a data breach over a 2-year period[5]

Data Security Solutions

You can see how minimizing the PPIs can benefit your bottom line. Because the DB2 Analytics Accelerator is an integrated component of DB2 for z/OS, users do not need separate credentials to access it. In other words, users don't get separate credentials to a separate data repository; rather, all access is controlled through DB2 for z/OS and through RACF security.

Conceptually, with the DB2 Analytics Accelerator, the z System operates analogous to a hybrid automobile. A hybrid automobile has a standard user interface comprised of a steering wheel with accelerator and brake pedals. But at any given moment, the hybrid automobile may be using its gasoline or electrical power source to meet the driver's current needs; the switching is automatic. In much the same way, the addition of the DB2 for z/OS with the DB2 Analytics Accelerator automatically routes data to the optimal processing engine to meet the users' needs—using a standardized interface without user intervention.

Beyond the automated optimization, the N300x hardware used with the DB2 Analytics Accelerator includes self-encrypting drives (SEDs). Also known as hardware-based full disk encryption, these drives implement an encryption algorithm in hardware within the disk drive. Using symmetric cypher AES256, all data written to the drive is encrypted at full interface speed before writing it to media and then decrypted before it is returned.

The symmetric disk encryption key (DEK) is unique to each drive and is stored in a secure, tamper-proof location on the drive, so it never leaves the drive. By default, the SED is in its unlocked state. During installation, an IBM field engineer will activate the encryption. Once this is done, data on the drive is always encrypted. Using the DEK and powering the disk on requires unlocking the DEK with the authentication encryption key (AEK), which means the drives cannot be unencrypted. For additional security, your service provider can manage or change the AEK encryption keys.

Since no system is immune, the inevitable question arises, "What if our DB2 for z/OS credentials are stolen?" To start, most z Systems customers already have sophisticated change management and access control policies in place through RACF and System Authorization Facility (SAF). However, you can deploy an additional layer of fraud detection by using a technology like IBM Guardium®.

With Guardium, you can perform outlier analysis to detect suspicious behavior against a norm for each user and block the transaction or thread, thus taking a more preventative and proactive approach to protecting data. In other words, Guardium can be used as a form of predictive whitelisting to identify anomalies in a user's behavior relating to sensitive data, and determine whether those anomalies may be related to a credential or data breach.

In addition to these new technologies, IBM also provides comprehensive data tools including discovery, classification, and vulnerability assessments as well as real-time monitoring, alerting, and blocking of suspicious behavior. These tools can be applied across many databases, data warehouses, off-the-shelf commercial applications, Hadoop clusters, and more. The reason is simple—a proactive approach to data security is far less expensive than the millions it can cost to resolve a data breach.

System Performance

Another reason for ETL proliferation is perceived performance improvements that could be realized by segmenting workloads based on data access characteristics. For example, OLTP workloads could remain on z Systems, while extremely CPU-intensive workloads could be run on an MPP system. This leads to multiple copies of the data for different access-method patterns, multiple instances of PPIs, increases in the number of data interfaces, application changes to point at different environments for different queries, and more.

While many believe the ETL structure is efficient, our clients tell us differently. Many organizations extract, transfer, and load data to a downstream data warehouse so they can execute long-running analytical queries to identify fraudulent and improperly rejected transactions.

One client reported it required over 24 hours to extract, transfer, and load content into the data warehouse, then 11 hours to execute their fraud-detection analytic suite. The 35 hours of latency not only increased their risk of financial losses due to fraud, it diminished customer satisfaction.

In another example, banks must continually assess and manage their market and asset liquidity risk to maintain minimum asset ratios for regulatory compliance and customer obligations. It is impossible to run analytics on real-time or near real-time data using legacy technologies alone. This forces banks to run nightly batch jobs to assess market and asset liquidity risk. These nightly runs are often too late to address liquidity events.

System Performance Solutions

Multiple banks have implemented the DB2 Analytics Accelerator and can now assess their trading risk positions in near real time rather than waiting for the overnight batch to run. This dramatically reduces each bank's liquidity risk and improves return on equity.

Another client, a large North American managed healthcare company, turned to the DB2 Analytics Accelerator because of its built-in MPP capabilities. As a result, they saw queries run up to 1908 times faster. Yet another client, an American investment management company, accelerated the delivery of canned reports using real-time data—realizing up to a 700 percent performance improvement in queries on intra-day activity and transaction volume.

In the past, it wasn't cost effective to offer this capability, or it required hard coding in applications as part of a development effort. Giving DB2 for z/OS the flexibility to run queries in DB2 for z/OS or on the DB2 Analytics Accelerator eliminates the need to manipulate data specifically for analytic workload performance or to manually segregate workloads across multiple interfaces to force specific access methods.

This can increase your system performance and simultaneously reduce your technology stack, helping improve your customer satisfaction by giving you visibility into what is happening in near real time and allowing more flexibility around ad hoc inquiries. The result is more analytics possibilities and bottom-line benefits without increasing your risk of data breach.

Data Archiving

With data quantities exploding, archiving has become an even more important component of your data management strategy. While active data that is still changing remains available in source systems, unchanging historical data is generally archived for future use.

Driven by cost, historical data is typically archived to less expensive, tape-based solutions. This includes archives that remain online due to auditing requirements and archives stored offline for more permanent storage.

While not being actively updated, the reality is that most archived data must still be analyzed by end users. For online archives, data access experiences a latency that eliminates real-time analysis options. For offline archives, analysis typically requires nightly batch processes to restore the data; this limits using this archived data to trend-type analyses. Figure 5 illustrates these flows.

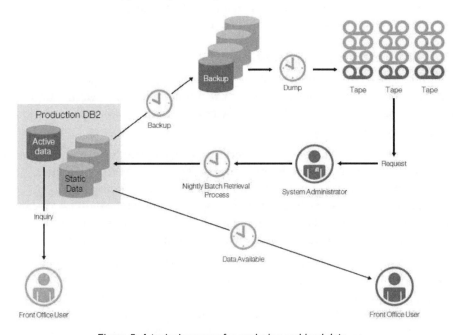

Figure 5: A typical process for analyzing archived data

Data Archiving Solutions

To address these challenges, the DB2 Analytics Accelerator includes an online archiving functionality called a high-performance storage saver. Using this functionality to move historical data into the DB2 Analytics Accelerator reduces the data volume in the DB2 for z/OS table; this means smaller indexes and smaller materialized query tables.

Just as important, moving this historical data into the DB2 Analytics Accelerator enables active analysis without any restore process. Access to both the historical and active data is managed through the same DB2 for z/OS interface and is protected through RACF security as opposed to interacting with the tape archive or copying the data to a separate DBMS and maintaining a separate data interface. And archive data durability is ensured through existing backup/recovery strategies.

By employing an HPSS, both active and online historical data are always available to the user for analysis and auditing purposes—with near-zero latency for online historical data queries. The DB2 for z/OS optimizer manages traffic and directs any queries that touch archived data to the DB2 Analytics Accelerator, while queries against strictly non-archived data follow the DB2 Analytics Accelerator's usual query-routing criteria. This means there will be near-zero CPU consumption associated with the analysis of the historical data.

In addition, you can realize cost savings by removing any batch jobs that take data from tape and load them in online tables. The size of online tables in DB2 for z/OS can then also be reduced by moving historical partitions to the DB2 Analytics Accelerator. A sample catalog query to uncover archiving opportunities in a DB2 for z/OS environment is available at *https://ibm.biz/BdX3gb*.

Performance, Security, and Savings

New technologies from IBM are transforming large-enterprise analytics. The traditional approach of using z Systems mainframes for mission-critical applications, and then extracting or replicating data from those systems to distributed databases for analysis, is losing its luster.

Now, DB2 for z/OS combined with the DB2 Analytics Accelerator gives you the ability to execute OLTP workloads and perform MPP-type queries on data— while that data remains within the DB2 for z/OS environment. That means you can obtain the competitive advantages that powerful analytics can provide—often with near-zero latency—without incurring the increased costs and elevated security risks associated with data administration, additional hardware, or ETL or replication approaches.

How IBM Can Help Your Bottom Line

For over a century, IBM has been pioneering technologies and providing services that help companies manage and mine their valuable business data. For 22 consecutive years, IBM has topped the annual list of US patent recipients— receiving a record 7,534 patents in 2014.[6] And by investing USD 24 billion in research and development (R&D) and acquisitions, IBM has established the world's deepest portfolio of big data and analytics technology that spans R&D, solutions, and software.[7]

Using this technical expertise, IBM has created a free cost-benefit analysis (CBA) workshop to help you visualize the hard dollar cost savings and efficiencies that can be gained by reducing data sprawl within your IT infrastructure. With the goal of avoiding data breach costs by improving security, while using a hard dollar justification, the CBA workshop considers all functional and non-functional requirements for the existing landing zones, data stores, and the feeds they support.

Using those requirements, the CBA workshop experts identify options for consolidating your IT infrastructure using solutions such as DB2 for z/OS sources, the IBM DB2 Analytics Accelerator, the IBM DB2 Analytics Accelerator Loader for z/OS, IBM Cognos® Business Intelligence, IBM SPSS® predictive analytics, Hadoop, additional mainframe hardware and software, as well as suggested deployment and quick start services. The experts then perform a CBA and value analysis using the proposed solution architecture to compare the cost of maintaining distributed databases against working with the data at the source, and finally can recommend a holistic approach to improve your technical architecture and help reduce your costs.

For More Information

To learn more about DB2 Analytics Accelerator, or to request your free cost-benefit analysis workshop, please contact your IBM sales representative or visit *https://ibm.biz/BdXTz4*.

Additionally, IBM Global Financing can help you acquire the IT solutions that your business needs in the most cost-effective and strategic way possible. For credit-qualified clients we can customize an IT financing solution to suit your business requirements, enable effective cash management, and improve your total cost of ownership. IBM Global Financing is your smartest choice to fund critical IT investments and propel your business forward. For more information, visit *ibm.com/financing*.

Notes

1. Poneman Institute. "2015 Cost of Data Breach Study: Global Analysis." May 2014.

2. This is based on an IBM internal total cost of ownership (TCO) calculation using the z Systems ETL Calculator App, which generates cost comparisons using customer-specific inputs. For this comparison, data usage was assumed to be 200 GB per day over a one-year period, using an ODS with one datamart with the z/OS operational software stack at medium complexity. More details on the ETL Calculator App, this specific example, and customer-specific savings can be obtained by contacting the IBM Eagle Team at *eagletco@us.ibm.com*.

3. IBM. "IBM z Systems Collocated Application Pricing for z/OS can improve the cost of deploying new z/OS applications." Accessed September 15, 2015. *www-01.ibm.com/ common/ssi/cgi-bin/ssialias?infotype=an&subtype=ca&appname=gpateam&supplier=897 &letternum=ENUS215-174*

4. Poneman Institute. "2014 Cost of Data Breach Study: Global Analysis." May 2014.

5. Poneman Institute. "2014 Cost of Data Breach Study: Global Analysis." May 2014.

6. IBM. "IBM Breaks U.S. Patent Record in 2014." Accessed August 18, 2015. *www-03.ibm.com/press/us/en/pressrelease/45793.wss*

7. IBM. "IBM Delivers New Big Data Capabilities on IBM Cloud Marketplace." Accessed August 25, 2015. *www-03.ibm.com/press/us/en/pressrelease/44188.wss*

Predictive Analytics Using IBM SPSS Modeler in DB2 for z/OS

by Jane Man, Lei Tian, and Liang Wang

Introduction

Why DB2 for z/OS Customers May Want to Use SPSS and the Business Value

DB2 for z/OS is an industry-recognized leader for mission-critical transactional systems. Unlike social data, transactional data is highly reliable, which makes it a valuable resource for analytics. To get insight from transactional data, in the past, mathematicians and developers used to work together on "offline data" to translate complicated mathematical algorithms into SQL statements, repeatedly testing to determine the best algorithms.

IBM SPSS Modeler is an industry-leading predictive analytics workbench. It provides a user-friendly GUI to build a predictive model based on built-in algorithms, test and find the best model, deploy predictive models, and do real-time scoring using the data stored in DB2 for z/OS. It uses the "SQL pushback" technique, which avoids extracting data from the database to Modeler to do scoring. It provides two ways to do scoring inside a database: with or without using the Server Scoring Adapter (Modeler UDFs). Other main characteristics are:

- Ease of use—visual, best-in-class predictive modeling
- Automation—for different types of users, from experienced data miners to business analysts
- Robust—provides a full set of data mining capabilities
- Deployment—fast development and deployment of models
- Scalable—optimized for in-database processing

Real-time scoring with DB2 for z/OS using IBM SPSS Modeler delivers the following business values:

- Delivers better, more profitable decisions, using the latest data, at the point of customer impact:
  - o Enables more informed customer interaction
  - o Improves fraud identification and prevention
- With improved accuracy, speed, and performance while reducing cost and complexity:
  - o Improves accuracy by scoring new and relevant data directly within the OLTP application
  - o Scales to large data volumes to improve accuracy of data models
  - o Delivers the performance needed to meet and exceed service-level agreements (SLAs) of OLTP applications
  - o Minimizes demand on network, hardware, software, and resources

The example in this article uses data in a sample table called DRUG1n, which you can create in your DB2 for z/OS system. The table contains information about patients given treatments for a particular illness and stores certain patient characteristics, such as cholesterol level and blood pressure.

The description of how to create and populate the table appears in the appendix on page 52. Alternatively, you can use your own data.

In the following sections, we will cover these topics:

- Setup and configuration
- Building a simple model
- Scoring inside DB2 for z/OS via Modeler UDF SQL
- Scoring inside DB2 for z/OS via pure SQL pushback
- Publishing the model into DB2 for z/OS
- Creating an SQL statement to do in database real-time scoring

Setup and Configuration

To enable SPSS support in DB2 10 for z/OS, you need the following items:

- IBM DB2 for z/OS 10 NFM with APARs to enable the PACK and UNPACK built-in functions:
  - o PM55928 for PACK/UNPACK preconditioning
  - o PM56631 for enabling
  - o PM74654 Scalability and performance improvements

- IBM SPSS Modeler with Scoring Adapter for zEnterprise v16.0 (PID 5655-AA8), which includes

  o FMID HHUMG10: IBM SPSS Modeler Server Scoring Adapter for DB2 for z/OS

- SPSS Modeler Client V16

- IBM SPSS OEM Connect64® for ODBC 6.1

The Scoring Adapter contains jobs to create the database, tables, and UDFs required by the Scoring Adapter; the job to define and set up the Workload Manager; and the job to bind the Scoring Adapter packages. See the Resources section on page 54 for more details.

Building a Simple Model Using Data Stored in DB2 for z/OS

The following steps illustrate how to build a simple model using Modeler (installed in Windows) and data stored in DB2 for z/OS. For Modeler to talk to DB2 for z/OS, we need to configure an ODBC data source name (DSN).

Step 1: Configure the ODBC DSN.

1. **Click Start > Control Panel**.

2. In Control Panel, find Administrative Tools, and **double-click** it.

3. Then **double-click** Data Source (ODBC).

4. In the ODBC Data Source Administrator dialog, **click** the Add button to add a new data source.

5. Drag the scroll bar to find IBM SPSS OEM 6.1 DB2 Wire Protocol, and **double-click** it as in Figure 1.

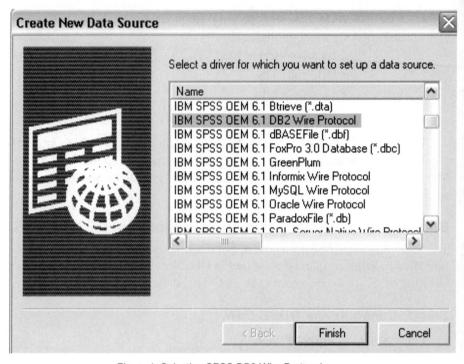

Figure 1: Selecting SPSS DB2 Wire Protocol

6. Enter the DSN, IP address, TCP port, location name, and the DB2 for z/OS collection you intend to connect to. Then **click** the Test Connect button.

The example in Figure 2 shows DB2 10 for z/OS as the data source name, zserveros.demos.ibm.com as the IP address, 5447 as the TCP port, EOSDB208 as the location name, and DSNT as the collection.

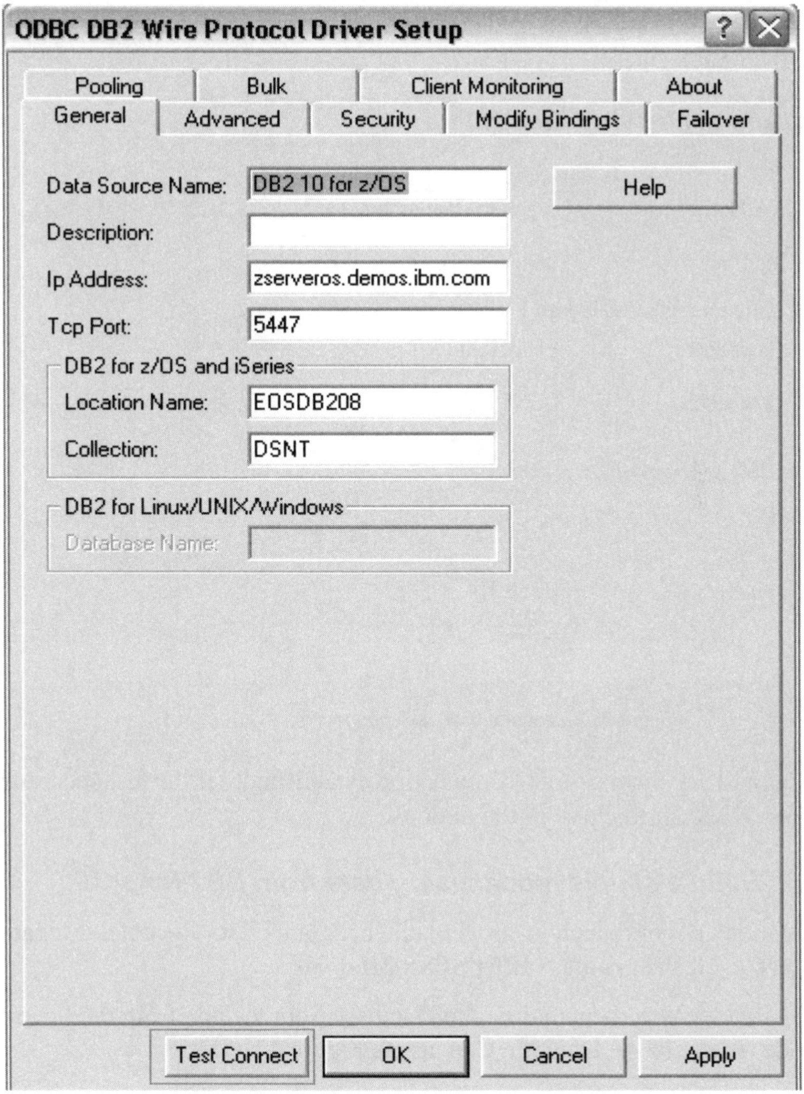

Figure 2: ODBC DB2 Wire Protocol Driver Setup

7. Enter the DB2 username and corresponding password, as shown as in Figure 3, then **click** OK.

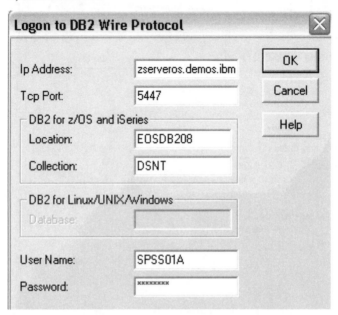

Figure 3: Testing the database connection

8. You will see the message "Connection established!" if the test succeeds. Then **click** OK to close all the dialogs.

Step 2: Build a simple model using data from DB2 for z/OS.

1. If Modeler Workbench is not yet launched, launch it. The default location is **Start** > **All Programs** > **IBM SPSS Modeler**.

2. In Modeler Workbench, drag the Database Source node from the Favorites node palette to the Diagram Canvas, as Figure 4 shows.

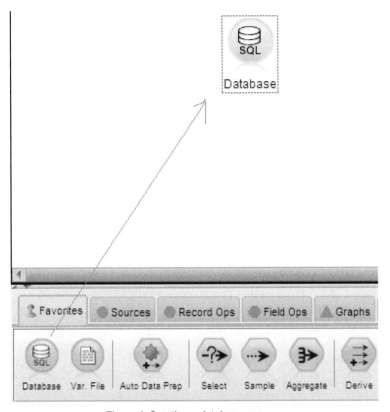

Figure 4: Creating a database source

3. **Double-click** the Database Source node icon in the Diagram Canvas to open the node properties dialog. Then in the Data source drop-down list, select `<Add new database connection... >` as shown in Figure 5.

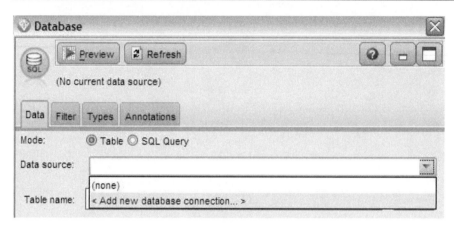

Figure 5: Adding a database connection

4. In the Database Connections dialog, select the "DB2 10 for z/OS" item (you must match this with the DSN you created in step 1 (g) above). Then enter the DB2 username and corresponding password, and **click** the Connect button, as in Figure 6. The new connection will be set up in the Connections table. **Click** the OK button to close this dialog.

Database Connections				
Server:	ioduser@ext5lnx.demos.ibm.com:28052			

Data sources:	Data source	Description
	DB2 10 for z/OS	DB2 10 on zserver.demos.ibm.com

Refresh

User name: SPSS01A

Password: ********

Connect

Connections:	Default	Save	Data source	Preset
	☐	☐	SPSS01A@DB2 10 for z/OS	

Figure 6: Setting up a database connection

5. In the database dialog (Figure 7), enter DRUG1n as the table name, then **click** the Preview button (upper left) to see the table content, as Figure 8 shows. (Note: We assume table DRUG1n is already created and populated inside

DB2 for z/OS. You can connect to any table you want to, but the following steps in this section are specifically for the DRUG1n table. For more information about how to load/insert data, please refer to the Appendix.)

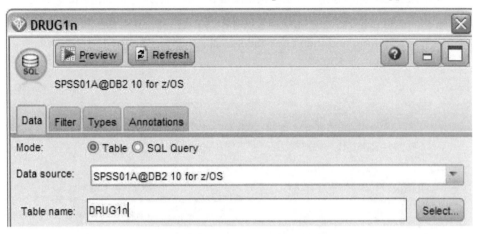

Figure 7: Selecting a table for analysis

Preview from DRUG1n Node (7 fields, 10 records)

File   Edit   Generate

| Table | Annotations | | | | | | |

	Age	Sex	BP	Cholesterol	Na	K	Drug
1	23	F	HIGH	HIGH	0.793	0.031	drugY
2	47	M	LOW	HIGH	0.739	0.056	drugC
3	47	M	LOW	HIGH	0.697	0.069	drugC
4	28	F	NORMAL	HIGH	0.564	0.072	drugX
5	61	F	LOW	HIGH	0.559	0.031	drugY
6	22	F	NORMAL	HIGH	0.677	0.079	drugX
7	49	F	NORMAL	HIGH	0.790	0.049	drugY
8	41	M	LOW	HIGH	0.767	0.069	drugC
9	60	M	NORMAL	HIGH	0.777	0.051	drugY
10	43	M	LOW	NORMAL	0.526	0.027	drugY

Figure 8: Previewing table content

As you can see in Figure 8, the DRUG1n table contains information about patient characteristics (age; gender; blood pressure; and cholesterol, sodium, and potassium levels) and what drug each individual is taking. We want to find out what characteristic (e.g., cholesterol level, blood pressure) is important in determining the drug the patient is taking.

Click the OK button of the table content preview dialog to close it.

6. In the node properties dialog, select the Types tab, click the Clear All Values button, and then click the Read Values button to read data types, as Figure 9 shows.

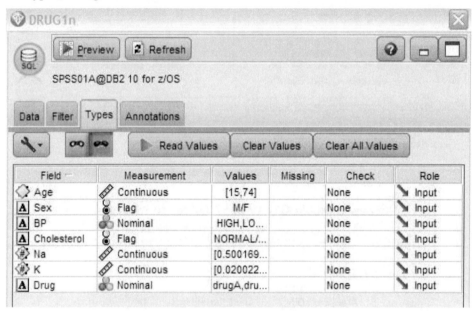

Figure 9: Refreshing the table data

7. We are going to build a classification model, which needs to mark one of the input fields as the Target field (also called the predictor field). In our example, modify the Role of the Drug field (column) to be Target, as in Figure 10. Then **click** OK to close the node properties dialog.

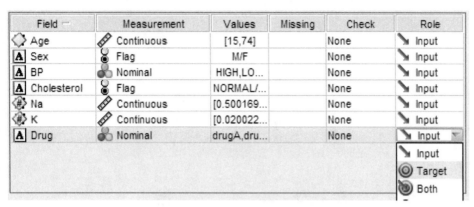

Field	Measurement	Values	Missing	Check	Role
◇ Age	✎ Continuous	[15,74]		None	⬊ Input
🅰 Sex	🎱 Flag	M/F		None	⬊ Input
🅰 BP	🔗 Nominal	HIGH,LO...		None	⬊ Input
🅰 Cholesterol	🎱 Flag	NORMAL/...		None	⬊ Input
⬡ Na	✎ Continuous	[0.500169...		None	⬊ Input
⬡ K	✎ Continuous	[0.020022...		None	⬊ Input
🅰 Drug	🔗 Nominal	drugA,dru...		None	⬊ Input ▾
					⬊ Input
					◎ Target
					🔘 Both

Figure 10: Marking the Target field

8. In Modeler Workbench, select the Modeling tab in the node palette panel, as in Figure 11.

Figure 11: Selecting the Modeling tab

9. Drag the CHAID node from the Modeling node palette to the Diagram Canvas. Each node icon in the Modeling node palette represents a modeling algorithm. In our example, the CHAID algorithm is one RULE INDUCTION algorithm, which derives a decision tree or a set of rules that attempt to describe distinct segments within the data in relation to a target field.

10. In the Diagram Canvas, **right-click** the DRUG1n node, in the context menu select Connect, and then click the CHAID node icon to set up a connection link, as in Figure 12.

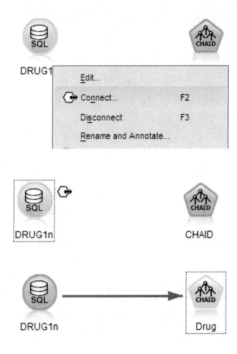

Figure 12: Connecting the table to an algorithm

11. At this point, we have constructed a simple stream containing one database source node and one modeling node. We could use this stream to build our CHAID model. **Right-click** the CHAID node, and select **Run** in its context menu, as in Figure 13. We will see a gold diamond-shaped icon generated, shown in Figure 14, which is the CHAID model (aka the CHAID nugget).

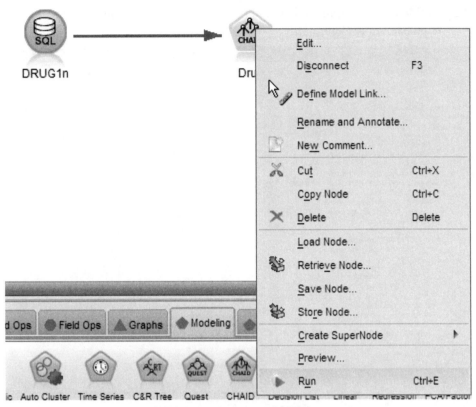

Figure 13: Running a stream

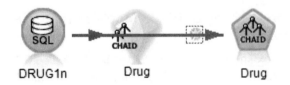

Figure 14: Creating a model

12. **Double-click** the golden diamond (CHAID model), and you will see the output shown in Figure 15.

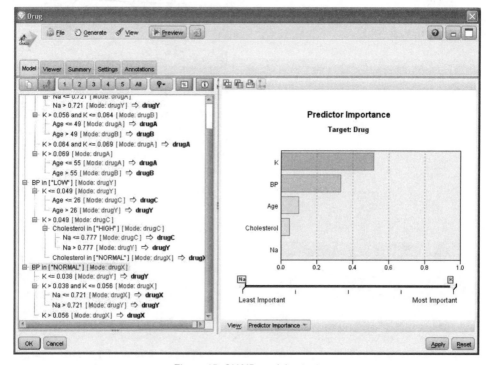

Figure 15: CHAID model output

The output in Figure 15 shows that K (potassium) is important in determining the drug that one person is taking, in the sample data in our database.

Scoring Inside DB2 for z/OS via Modeler UDF (Server Scoring Adapter)

We will use a pre-existing stream file (RenewalModel_IOD.str) to do scoring. In this stream file, a renewal model is used to predict the likelihood that a policy holder will renew his or her policy. (You can download the stream file at *www.ibm.com/developerworks/data/library/techarticle/dm-1505predictive-spss-db2zos/index.html*, Downloads section.)

1. Open RenewalModel_IOD.str in Modeler Workbench via **File** > **Open Stream**.

2. **Click** the Analysis node in the first branch (it should become highlighted), then **click** the SQL Preview button in the Modeler Workbench tool bar, as in Figure 16.

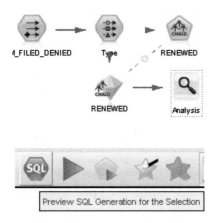

Figure 16: Previewing the generated SQL statement

SQL generation is now started. In regard to the Analysis node as terminal node, you will notice all upstream (previous) node icons become purple (Figure 17 shows these icons), and the generated RENEWED model nugget become purple as well, which means that the scoring is done inside database.

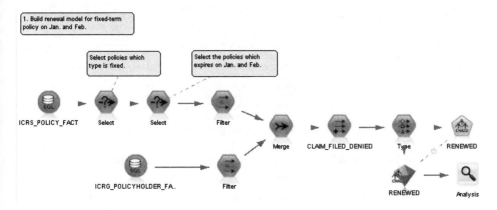

Figure 17: Generating the new SQL statement for scoring

3. The SQL Preview button is used to see the possible SQL generation for a stream execution. Sometimes we want to know in advance how many operations can be pushed back; in such cases, we simply click the SQL Preview button to have a look. The advantage of this is that the generated

SQL expressions are not executed by clicking the SQL Preview button, which saves execution effort and also prevents execution impact.

4. To view the generated SQL statements, click the Show stream messages button at the middle bottom of Modeler Workbench.

Figure 18: Show stream messages button

The stream properties dialog will then open, as shown in Figure 19.

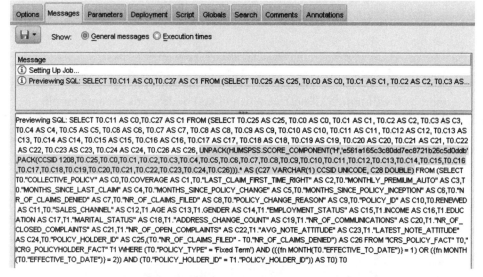

Figure 19: The SQL statement generated for scoring

In Figure 19, the Modeler Scoring UDF SQL statement is highlighted to make it easy to distinguish. The UDF name is HUMSPSS.SCORE_ COMPONENT; this UDF works together with the DB2 for z/OS PACK/ UNPACK built-in function to ensure a successful scoring. The UDF package needs to be installed into DB2 for z/OS before we can use it. (Refer to the DB2 for z/OS Modeler UDF Installation documentation for more details.)

By default, Modeler will generate UDF SQL to score using the UDF Server Scoring Adapter in Modeler product, if it is installed, as Figure 20 shows.

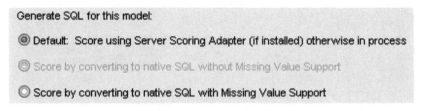

Figure 20: Options for generating SQL

The above option exists in the CHAID model nugget. To view or change the SQL-generation option, **double-click** the RENEWED model nugget and **click** the Settings tab.

If you can't see any UDF SQL in the Messages tab of the Stream properties dialog, **click** the **Options** > **Logging and Status** sub-tab of the same Stream properties dialog, and make sure Logging options is checked, as shown in Figure 21.

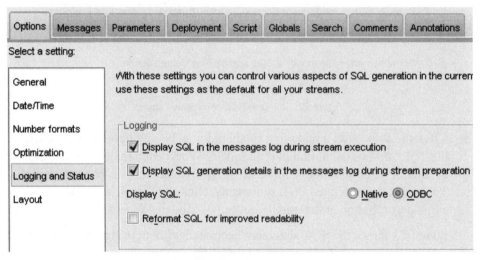

Figure 21: Setting up the logging properties

Scoring Inside DB2 for z/OS via SQL Pushback

As mentioned, we can also do scoring without using the Modeler UDFs. As in the previous section, we will use the same first branch of the stream (RenewalModel_IOD.str) to score via pure SQL pushback.

1. **Double-click** the RENEWED model nugget, click the Settings tab, then modify the Generate SQL for this model option from Default to Score by converting to native SQL with Missing Value support, as in Figure 22. Then **click** the OK button.

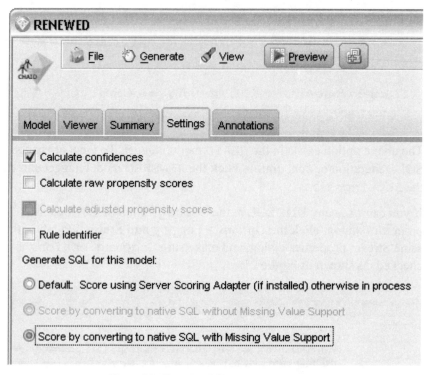

Figure 22: Changing SQL-generation settings

2. **Click** the `Analysis` node first (it should now be highlighted), then **click** the `SQL Preview` button in the Modeler Workbench toolbar to start SQL generation. You will notice all upstream (previous) node icons turn purple. To look at the generated SQL statements, **click** the `Show stream messages` button at the middle bottom of Modeler Workbench.

Figure 23 shows the SQL statement generated without using Modeler UDFs.

Message
ⓘ Previewing SQL: SELECT 1 AS C0,T0.C0 AS C1,T0.C1 AS C2,COUNT(*) AS C3,T0.C0 AS C4,T0.C1 AS C5 FROM (SELECT T0.C2 AS C0,(CA...
ⓘ Previewing SQL: SELECT COUNT(*) AS C0 FROM (SELECT T0."MONTHS_SINCE_POLICY_CHANGE" AS C0,T0."MONTHS_SINCE_POLICY_IN...

Previewing SQL: SELECT 1 AS C0,T0.C0 AS C1,T0.C1 AS C2,COUNT(*) AS C3,T0.C0 AS C4,T0.C1 AS C5 FROM (SELECT T0.C2 AS C0,(CASE \
HEN ((T0.C0 <= 13.0) AND (T0.C0 > 0.0)) THEN (CASE WHEN (T0.C4 <= 21.0) THEN '1' WHEN ((T0.C4 <= 24.0) AND (T0.C4 > 21.0)) THEN '1' WH
N (T0.C4 > 49.0) THEN '1' ELSE (CASE WHEN (T0.C3 = 'Web') THEN '1' ELSE '1' END) END) WHEN (T0.C0 > 13.0) THEN (CASE WHEN (T0.C9 > 1.0
THEN '1' ELSE '1' END) ELSE (CASE WHEN (T0.C4 <= 21.0) THEN (CASE WHEN (T0.C11 <= 3.0) THEN (CASE WHEN (T0.C8 > 5.0) THEN '0' ELSE
' END) ELSE (CASE WHEN (T0.C1 > 47.0) THEN '1' ELSE '0' END) END) WHEN ((T0.C4 <= 24.0) AND (T0.C4 > 21.0)) THEN (CASE WHEN ((T0.C6 =
'Medical Leave') OR (T0.C6 = 'Unemployed')) THEN (CASE WHEN (T0.C8 > 4.0) THEN '0' ELSE '1' END) ELSE (CASE WHEN (T0.C11 <= 3.0) THEN
ELSE '1' END) END) WHEN ((T0.C4 <= 29.0) AND (T0.C4 > 24.0)) THEN (CASE WHEN (T0.C11 > 4.0) THEN '1' ELSE (CASE WHEN (T0.C7 <= 3407
.0) THEN '1' ELSE '1' END) END) WHEN ((T0.C4 <= 40.0) AND (T0.C4 > 29.0)) THEN (CASE WHEN ((T0.C11 <= 6.0) AND (T0.C11 > 3.0)) THEN (CA
SE WHEN (T0.C1 <= 47.0) THEN '1' ELSE '1' END) WHEN ((T0.C11 <= 11.0) AND (T0.C11 > 6.0)) THEN '1' WHEN (T0.C11 > 11.0) THEN (CASE WH
N (T0.C10 <= 0.0) THEN '1' ELSE '1' END) ELSE (CASE WHEN (T0.C1 > 76.0) THEN '1' ELSE (CASE WHEN ((((T0.C6 = 'Disabled') OR (T0.C6 = 'Med
al Leave')) OR (T0.C6 = 'Unemployed')) THEN '1' ELSE '1' END) END) END) WHEN (T0.C4 > 49.0) THEN (CASE WHEN (T0.C11 <= 3.0) THEN (CASE
WHEN ((((T0.C6 = 'Disabled') OR (T0.C6 = 'Medical Leave')) OR (T0.C6 = 'Retired')) OR (T0.C6 = 'Unemployed')) THEN '0' ELSE '0' END) ELSE (CA
SE WHEN (T0.C7 <= 34075.0) THEN '1' ELSE '1' END) END) ELSE (CASE WHEN (T0.C11 <= 0.0) THEN (CASE WHEN ((T0.C8 = 6.0) AND (T0.C8 >

Figure 23: Scoring the SQL statement without using Modeler UDFs

You will notice a longer and more complex SQL statement compared with the SQL statement generated using the Server Scoring Adapter. This is because we are generating pure SQL this time. The pure SQL pushback uses only the database's built-in SQL expressions and functions to score data. The model-scoring algorithm itself is translated into corresponding SQL expressions (our RENEWED model example includes many CASE WHEN ... THEN ... statements, as the model contains a lot of rules), which means many more SQL expressions are generated for the model-scoring algorithm. The UDF SQL example is different, because it contains only one UDF to represent the entire model-scoring algorithm.

One advantage of UDF SQL is that it supports more models than pure SQL pushback supports. Most of the models generated in Modeler Workbench support scoring via UDF SQL, while only a few of them support scoring via pure SQL pushback. Typically, pure SQL pushback is faster when a model can be described with a few SQL expressions (the model-scoring algorithm logic is simple—e.g., the Linear Regression model), but UDF SQL will outperform SQL pushback when a model is more complicated (e.g., the Neural Net model).

Publishing the Model into DB2 for z/OS

Modeler Workbench provides a way to publish an SPSS model into DB2 for z/OS and return an example SQL statement template, which can be used to do real-time scoring.

We will use the same first branch of the stream (`RenewalModel_ IOD.str`) to show how to publish a model to DB2 for z/OS.

1. **Double-click** the RENEWED model nugget to open the model properties dialog, then select the `File` menu, and select the `Publish for Server Scoring Adapter...` option, as in Figure 24.

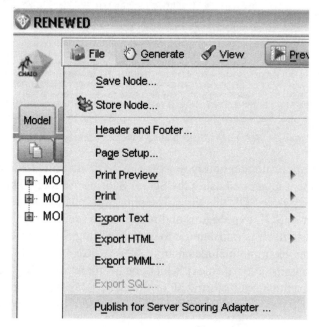

Figure 24: Selecting to publish for Server Scoring Adapter

2. In the opened dialog, shown in Figure 25, select the corresponding database connection you would like to publish. Here, it is `SPSS01A@DB2 10 for z/OS`.

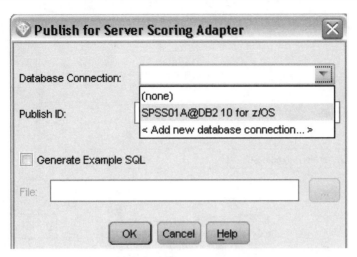

Figure 25: Selecting the target database

3. Then enter a proper publish ID string to identify the model, as in Figure 26. The publish ID is used as the model reference in application SQL statements. We use RENEWED_MODEL as the publish ID for our example.

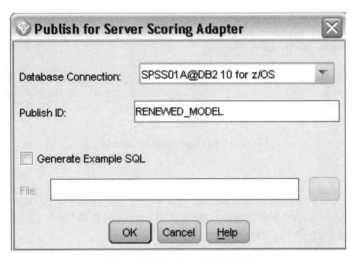

Figure 26: Creating a Publish ID

4. Select the Generate Example SQL check box. Then **click** the Browse for file button to open a file chooser, and after that choose a new filename (e.g., RENEWED) to store the example SQL, as shown in Figure 27.

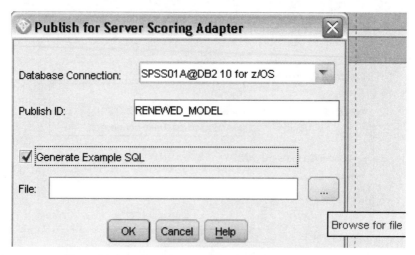

Figure 27: Selecting a file location to store the SQL statements

You can **click** the Desktop button in the File Chooser dialog to store the corresponding example SQL file on the desktop (see Figure 28). Then **click** Save to close the File Chooser dialog, and **click** OK to close the Publish dialog.

Figure 28: Storing output on the desktop

5. After a few seconds, you will find that a new file with the name you specified in step 4 has been generated; its content will be displayed, similar to that shown in Figure 29.

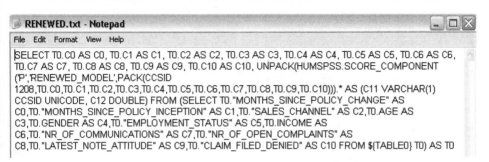

Figure 29: SQL template after publishing a model

This is the sample SQL template returned for us to use in other applications. You can see that the publish ID RENEWED_MODEL that we entered previously appears in the example SQL template. Also notice in the generated SQL template the internal nested SQL statement that contains $(TABLE0). In the next section, we will see how to replace the corresponding part of the example SQL template for a real-time in-database scoring.

6. To verify that we have published our model successfully, issue the SELECT statement, as in Listing 1.

```
SELECT * FROM HUMSPSS.PUBLISHED_COMPONENTS WHERE ID =
'RENEWED_MODEL'
```

Listing 1: SQL statement to verify a successful model publication

Figure 30 illustrates a possible output for Listing 1. A HASHED_ID is generated for each successfully published model.

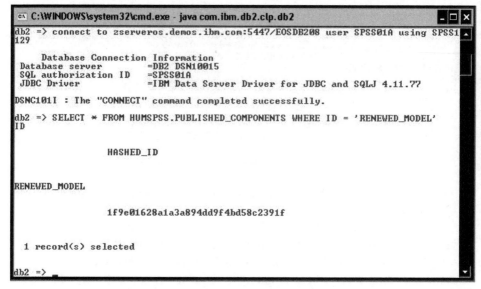

Figure 30: Output for a successful model publication

Creating an SQL Statement to Perform In-Database Real-time Scoring

In this section, we will use the model we published in the previous section to perform in-database real-time scoring. Listing 2 shows the returned example SQL template from the previous section (RENEWED.txt).

```
SELECT T0.C0 AS C0, T0.C1 AS C1, T0.C2 AS C2, T0.C3 AS C3, T0.C4
AS C4, T0.C5 AS C5, T0.C6 AS C6, T0.C7 AS C7, T0.C8 AS C8, T0.C9
AS C9, T0.C10 AS C10,
UNPACK(HUMSPSS.SCORE_COMPONENT('P','RENEWED_MODEL',PACK(CCSID
1208,T0.C0,T0.C1,T0.C2,T0.C3,T0.C4,T0.C5,T0.C6,T0.C7,T0.C8,T0.C9,T
0.C10))).* AS (C11 VARCHAR(1) CCSID UNICODE, C12 DOUBLE) FROM
(SELECT T0."MONTHS_SINCE_POLICY_CHANGE" AS
C0,T0."MONTHS_SINCE_POLICY_INCEPTION" AS C1,T0."SALES_CHANNEL" AS
C2,T0.AGE AS C3,T0.GENDER AS C4,T0."EMPLOYMENT_STATUS" AS
C5,T0.INCOME AS C6,T0."NR_OF_COMMUNICATIONS" AS
C7,T0."NR_OF_OPEN_COMPLAINTS" AS C8,T0."LATEST_NOTE_ATTITUDE" AS
C9,T0."CLAIM_FILED_DENIED" AS C10 FROM ${TABLE0} T0) AS T0
```

Listing 2: SQL template after a successful model publication

The type of SQL shown in our example is flexible enough to integrate with various kinds of business database applications. In real applications, we would need to replace the bold section in Listing 2 with real records data (usually one row or a few rows). Following are several examples.

1. Using the data that already exists in DB2 for z/OS, we can replace the bold part of the SQL statement in Listing 2 with that shown in Listing 3 to analyze a specific age group (e.g., AGE=21). Figure 31 shows the complete SQL statement.

```
SELECT T0."MONTHS_SINCE_POLICY_CHANGE" AS
C0,T0."MONTHS_SINCE_POLICY_INCEPTION" AS C1,T0."SALES_CHANNEL" AS
C2,T0.AGE AS C3,T0.GENDER AS C4,T0."EMPLOYMENT_STATUS" AS
C5,T0.INCOME AS C6,T0."NR_OF_COMMUNICATIONS" AS
C7,T0."NR_OF_OPEN_COMPLAINTS" AS C8,T0."LATEST_NOTE_ATTITUDE" AS
C9,T0."CLAIM_FILED_DENIED" AS C10 FROM ICRG_VIEW1 T0 WHERE
T0."AGE" = 21
```

Listing 3: SQL statement (partial) to analyze a specific age group

```
db2 => SELECT T0.C0 AS C0, T0.C1 AS C1, T0.C2 AS C2, T0.C3 AS C3, T0.C4 AS C4, T
0.C5 AS C5, T0.C6 AS C6, T0.C7 AS C7, T0.C8 AS C8, T0.C9 AS C9, T0.C10 AS C10, U
NPACK(HUMSPSS.SCORE_COMPONENT('P','RENEWED_MODEL',PACK(CCSID 1208,T0.C0,T0.C1,T0
.C2,T0.C3,T0.C4,T0.C5,T0.C6,T0.C7,T0.C8,T0.C9,T0.C10))).* AS (C11 VARCHAR(1) CCS
ID UNICODE, C12 DOUBLE) FROM (SELECT T0."MONTHS_SINCE_POLICY_CHANGE" AS C0,T0."M
ONTHS_SINCE_POLICY_INCEPTION" AS C1,T0."SALES_CHANNEL" AS C2,T0.AGE AS C3,T0.GEN
DER AS C4,T0."EMPLOYMENT_STATUS" AS C5,T0.INCOME AS C6,T0."NR_OF_COMMUNICATIONS"
 AS C7,T0."NR_OF_OPEN_COMPLAINTS" AS C8,T0."LATEST_NOTE_ATTITUDE" AS C9,T0."CLAI
M_FILED_DENIED" AS C10 FROM ICRG_VIEW1 T0 WHERE T0."AGE" = 21) AS T0_
```

Figure 31: Complete SQL statement to analyze a specific age group

You may see the following scoring result (Figure 32):

```
18          37            Agent                                              21
 F     Unemployed                                        0                   1
     0          1               15        1   0.9979674796747966
21          69            Web                                                21
 M     Unemployed                                        0                    4
     0          0                3        1   0.9979674796747966
   230 record(s) selected


db2 =>
```

Figure 32: Scoring output (partial) for age group 21

Figure 32 shows the partial output for our analysis. There are 230 records that have AGE=21. The last two columns are the scoring output, which indicates the likelihood that a policyholder will renew his or her policy.

2. Similarly, using the data that already exists in DB2 for z/OS, we can replace the bold part of the SQL statement in Listing 2 to that shown in Listing 4 to analyze a specific policyholder (e.g., POLICY_HOLDER_ID=1032121).

```
SELECT T0."MONTHS_SINCE_POLICY_CHANGE" AS
C0,T0."MONTHS_SINCE_POLICY_INCEPTION" AS C1,T0."SALES_CHANNEL" AS
C2,T0.AGE AS C3,T0.GENDER AS C4,T0."EMPLOYMENT_STATUS" AS
C5,T0.INCOME AS C6,T0."NR_OF_COMMUNICATIONS" AS
C7,T0."NR_OF_OPEN_COMPLAINTS" AS C8,T0."LATEST_NOTE_ATTITUDE" AS
C9,T0."CLAIM_FILED_DENIED" AS C10 FROM ICRG_VIEW1 T0 WHERE
T0."POLICY_HOLDER_ID" = 1032121
```

Listing 4: SQL statement (partial) to analyze a specific policyholder

Figure 33 is the scoring output for policyholder 1032121. The scoring result (C11=$R-RENEWED=1, C12=$RC-RENEWED=0.9796) means the policyholder (POLICY_HOLDER_ID=1032121) is likely to renew his/her policy, with the confidence or renewal probability of 0.9796.

```
db2 => SELECT T0.C0 AS C0, T0.C1 AS C1, T0.C2 AS C2, T0.C3 AS C3, T0.C4 AS C4, T
0.C5 AS C5, T0.C6 AS C6, T0.C7 AS C7, T0.C8 AS C8, T0.C9 AS C9, T0.C10 AS C10, U
NPACK(HUMSPSS.SCORE_COMPONENT('P','RENEWED_MODEL',PACK(CCSID 1208,T0.C0,T0.C1,T0
.C2,T0.C3,T0.C4,T0.C5,T0.C6,T0.C7,T0.C8,T0.C9,T0.C10))).* AS (C11 VARCHAR(1) CCS
ID UNICODE, C12 DOUBLE) FROM (SELECT T0."MONTHS_SINCE_POLICY_CHANGE" AS C0,T0."M
ONTHS_SINCE_POLICY_INCEPTION" AS C1,T0."SALES_CHANNEL" AS C2,T0.AGE AS C3,T0.GEN
DER AS C4,T0."EMPLOYMENT_STATUS" AS C5,T0.INCOME AS C6,T0."NR_OF_COMMUNICATIONS"
 AS C7,T0."NR_OF_OPEN_COMPLAINTS" AS C8,T0."LATEST_NOTE_ATTITUDE" AS C9,T0."CLAI
M_FILED_DENIED" AS C10 FROM ICRG_VIEW1 T0 WHERE T0."POLICY_HOLDER_ID" = 1032121)
 AS T0
C0          C1            C2                                           C3
 C4   C5                                                      C6        C7
 C8          C9              C10          C11 C12
0          87              Call Center                      99747      46
 M     Employed                                                         9
     0          0                9        1   0.979633401221996
   1 record(s) selected


db2 =>
```

Figure 33: Scoring output for policyholder 1032121

3. The previous two examples are based on the fact that the real data already exists in DB2 for z/OS. For data that does not exist in DB2 for z/OS, we could also use the Modeler UDF (SCORE_COMPONENT, registered in DB2 for z/OS) to do real-time scoring.

Listing 5 shows the SQL statement used to see how likely a particular person whose data does not exist in the database (e.g., age 21, unemployed) will renew his or her policy.

```
SELECT
UNPACK(HUMSPSS.SCORE_COMPONENT('P','RENEWED_MODEL',PACK(CCSID
1208, INT(0), INT(4), 'Call Center', INT(21), 'M', 'Unemployed',
INT(0), INT(3), INT(0), INT(0), INT(5)))).* AS (RENEWED VARCHAR(1)
CCSID UNICODE, CONFIDENCE DOUBLE) FROM SYSIBM.SYSDUMMY1
```

Listing 5: SQL statement to do scoring for records not in the database

Figure 34 shows the output for Listing 5. The scoring result (RENEWED=0, CONFIDENCE=0.545) means the incoming real-time data value has a high churn risk, with a churn probability of 0.545.

```
db2 => SELECT UNPACK(HUMSPSS.SCORE_COMPONENT('P','RENEWED_MODEL',PACK(CCSID 1208
, INT(0), INT(4), 'Call Center', INT(21), 'M', 'Unemployed', INT(0), INT(3), INT
(0), INT(0), INT(5)))).* AS (RENEWED VARCHAR(1) CCSID UNICODE, CONFIDENCE DOUBLE
) FROM SYSIBM.SYSDUMMY1
RENEWED CONFIDENCE
0       0.5449101796407181
  1 record(s) selected

db2 =>
```

Figure 34: Scoring output for a record that does not exist in database

The first invocation of UDF real-time scoring may take more time because there is no memory-cached model, but subsequent real-time scoring of the same model (identified by the publish ID) will become faster over time.

Summary

This article discussed how to build a predictive model using IBM SPSS Modeler Workbench with data stored in DB2 for z/OS. We demonstrated how to do scoring using Modeler UDF and SQL pushback. We also showed how to publish a model into DB2 for z/OS, and how to create a SQL statement to do in-database real-time scoring.

Acknowledgments

Thanks to Robin Sun and Susan Malaika for their comments and assistance with this paper.

Appendix: Load/Insert Data into DB2 for z/OS

1. If Modeler Workbench is not yet launched, launch the Modeler Workbench. The default location is **Start** > **All Programs** > **IBM SPSS Modeler**.

2. In Modeler Workbench, drag the `Var. File Source` node from the `Favorites` node palette to the Diagram Canvas, setting its data path as in Figure A (the default location of `DRUG1n` in Modeler 16 is `C:\Program Files\IBM\SPSS\Modeler\16\Demos`). Then **click** `Open` to set the data, and **click** `OK` to close the dialog.

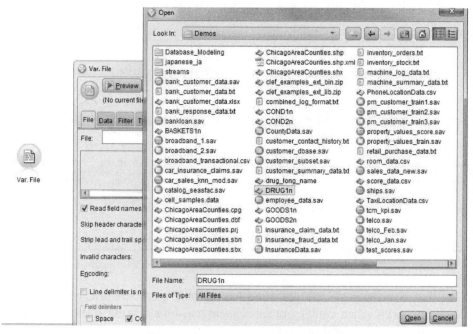

Figure A: Creating a Var. File source

3. In Modeler Workbench, drag the `Database export` node from the `Favorites` node palette to the Diagram Canvas, connecting the `Var .File source` node to the `Database export` node, as in Figure B.

DRUG1n

Database

Figure B: Database export node

4. **Double-click** the Database export node icon in the Diagram Canvas to open the node properties dialog. Then in the Data source drop-down list, select the existing connection "DB2 10 for z/OS" item and set the Export table name (e.g., DRUG1n), as shown in Figure C. Then **click** OK to close the node dialog.

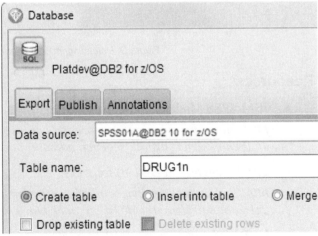

Figure C: Database export node setting

5. **Right-click** the Database export node, and in the context menu select Run to upload/insert data, as Figure D shows.

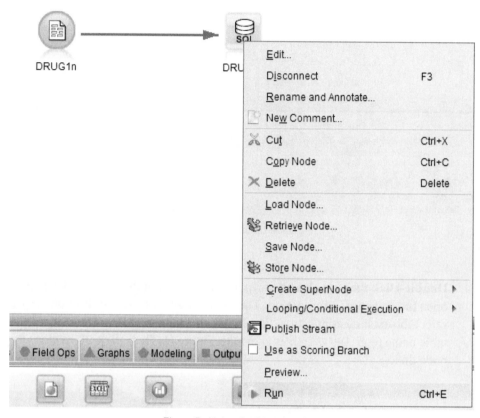

Figure D: Uploading/inserting data

Resources

- IBM SPSS Modeler 16 Scoring Adapter Installation:

  ftp://public.dhe.ibm.com/software/analytics/spss/documentation/modeler/16.0/en/modeler_install_scoring_adapter_book.pdf

- PACK function in DB2 10 for z/OS:

  http://publib.boulder.ibm.com/infocenter/dzichelp/v2r2/topic/com.ibm.db2z10.doc.sqlref/src/tpc/db2z_bif_pack.htm

- UNPACK function in DB2 10 for z/OS:

  http://publib.boulder.ibm.com/infocenter/dzichelp/v2r2/topic/com.ibm.db2z10.doc.sqlref/src/tpc/db2z_bif_unpack.htm

Maximizing Mobile Initiatives with IBM DB2 for z/OS

Banking on a Mobile Strategy with IBM DB2 for z/OS

by Surekha Parekh and Mark Simmonds

Introduction

Whether in a financial boom or an economic downturn, managing personal finances remains a high priority for everyone. Consumers ask themselves whether they should be investing, cutting back, diversifying, making that purchase decision, or putting the money aside for later. Banking and financial organizations that manage money are under increasing pressure to cut costs and reduce risks while both increasing the "wallet share" of existing customers and growing the customer base.

If there is one industry that has the stigma of being old and boring, it would have to be banking. However, a global trend of deregulation has opened up many new businesses to the banks. Coupling that with technological developments like Internet banking, ATMs, online banking and mobile applications, the banking industry is obviously trying its hardest to shed its lackluster image. In addition, every day there are more and more challenges facing the banking industry.

The Need for Banks to Become Customer Centric

The banking industry is under enormous pressure to understand its customers' needs and wants and to increase revenue streams. The time has come for banks to act in a less traditional fashion and become more customer centric. Banks like yours need to shape strategy according to customer demand. This requires encouraging more mobile interactions, making transactions more interactive, and delivering more "right now" experiences to give customers want they want when then want it.

Maintaining customer satisfaction has become a key area of where banks can differentiate themselves, because consumers have many choices when it comes to banking. Your future success depends on how well you listen to customers. You control whether they stay with you and buy more services—or whether low loyalty levels cause them to bank elsewhere.

1. Understanding the business value of customers

   In the banking industry, connecting consistently with customers will require that banks like yours understand the demographics of your markets, including the characteristics that define your best customers. That means learning which products and services they are willing to pay for. It also means developing the right distribution channels, as consumers increasingly use more than one channel. One recent study found that consumers handle their four top banking activities—bill paying, viewing balances and transactions, viewing statements, and transferring money—more frequently on the Internet than by any other channel.[1]

2. Reducing cost

   At the same time as they work to improve customer satisfaction, banks are under more and more pressure to reduce costs. One of the ways financial institutions have tried to reduce costs and increase customer service levels is to push high-volume, low-cost transactions through lower-cost delivery channels like mobile and Web. This has been a successful strategy, and has given branch tellers and staff the time to handle more valuable customer-centric services. However, with new technology and increasing consumer demands, banks will likely be under continually increasing pressure to reduce costs.

3. Security

   This is a key area of concern both for banks and their customers. The increased use of social and mobile channels combined with the organization's need to quickly handle increasing volumes of big data can often attract undesirable elements who may attempt to breach the data. Cyber thieves and vandals, combined with increasing regulatory demands on banks, are making the emphasis on data security more critical than ever before.

This paper discusses how and why mobile computing solutions built around IBM® z Systems™ and IBM DB2® for z/OS® can help banks deliver on these challenges. These solutions can provide improved customer reach, better customer service, deeper business insights, as well as help reduce costs, improve awareness of security needs, and help banks gain a competitive advantage.

The Mobile Tipping Point

The Web and the Internet brought many benefits to customers by offering 24 x 7 access to shopping, banking, social media, and more by using a PC from the convenience of the customer's own home.

The introduction of smart mobile devices, however, has fundamentally changed the business landscape. With an always-on device that is never out of arm's reach, customers, partners and employees all now have anytime, anywhere, any-device access to information. That access gives virtually everyone the possibility to make decisions and take action faster than ever.

Business is changing how mobile computing gets deployed, secured, and analyzed. Organizations are finding new ways to leverage mobile data analytics, which adds time-sensitivity and location data of each transaction. And they're applying those insights for greater influence over each user's decisions and actions. It's a win/win for both consumers and businesses.

For many, the mobile device has now become the primary computing platform for personal and business use, with the ability to have both workloads coexisting on the same device. With so many devices in use, data through the mobile channel is rapidly growing at an estimated 61 percent.[2] Banks now need to store, process, manage, secure, and analyze this tsunami of mobile data with little or no impact on existing workloads and service levels.

> Mass adoption and rise in mobile devices will drive data through the mobile channel to increase 61 percent compound annual growth rate (CAGR) 2013 – 2018.[3]

Mobile also adds two very important dimensions that create more insight and understanding of consumers: geographic location and time-sensitivity. Mobile computing as it relates to banking is no longer only focused on a consumer making a transaction using a smartphone. It is also important to know the consumer's location and buying patterns. With these insights, it becomes easier to anticipate the customer's next move so the bank can send a timely, relevant offer to that smartphone. At the same time, it is critical to protect your customers' interests by helping reduce fraud and risk in every transaction.

As more users and businesses become actively engaged, mobility has evolved beyond being simply another channel for connecting. It can also help create deep digital personal relationships that can become the primary channel for the business. However, the degree of business success depends on a great end-user experience. Everything has to fit together smoothly, from the mobile application right through to the technical infrastructure that supports it.

Mobile Redefines the Business and Responsibilities

Not only has mobile changed the business landscape, it can also impact executive responsibilities:

- **CIO and CTO**—These roles are faced with meeting rapidly evolving omni-channel demands, faster and more cost-effectively. They must implement "bring your own device" (BYOD) policies and manage sensitive data security, regardless of device. These officers must also manage multi-platform mobile complexities by selecting technologies that can be used to quickly develop and deploy high-quality mobile apps on multiple mobile platforms. Their primary objective is to seamlessly connect mobile apps to enterprise data and services to create a rich, fully featured mobile experience.

- **CMO**—Marketers need to drive top-line growth through optimized digital and mobile experiences that will enhance customer engagement and conversion. By gaining insight into mobile behaviors and quantifying business impact, the CMO can improve customer service resolution and drive loyalty.

- **CSO or CISO**—This role must defend the organization from threats posed by increased mobile connections. This includes protecting mobile devices and mobile data as well as guarding the corporate network. By helping ensure secure access and safeguarding mobile apps, this officer can deliver outstanding user experience without compromising security.

IBM z Systems and IBM DB2 for z/OS can help address all of these needs.

Banking Your Business on a Mobile Strategy—the DB2 for z/OS Advantage

IBM DB2 for z/OS and CICS are respectively the primary database and transaction manager behind many of the world's banking and financial institutions for high-volume transactions and complex analytics workloads. Together they provide the ability to securely store, process and manage transactions, along with capabilities to scale performance without impacting existing workloads. Furthermore, in the fast-moving mobile world, information that is an hour old may be too outdated to help bank employees identify potential fraud. Or it may be too stale to give the bank an opportunity to up-sell and cross-sell other services to customers.

Mobile workloads activity is often unpredictable, potentially increasing transaction volumes by as much as 50 percent with little or no warning. A world event, something viral on social media, a potential fraud, a disaster, Black Friday sales—any of these can cause unexpected massive peaks in demand. The IBM z

Systems platform and DB2 for z/OS are well suited to handle both the anticipated rapid growth of mobile workloads and the massive spikes in demand that can occur at any time. In fact, the recently released IBM z13™ platform is built specifically for the mobile era, delivering up to 36 percent better response time with up to 61 percent better throughput—while helping lower the cost per mobile transaction from 17 percent to 37 percent.[4]

Mobile banking customers expect the ability to check their balance anytime, anywhere before making a purchase. With the capability to electronically deposit a check by uploading a photo, or transfer money across international boundaries and pay bills, the need to physically visit a bank is diminishing. However, a less-than-optimal user interface or unpleasant online banking experience can be reason enough for customers to take their business elsewhere. This makes the importance of managing customers' digital relationship with the bank more important than ever.

The need for security, reliability and availability—along with the need to support huge volumes of connections, transactions and data—is why many organizations, including the Nationwide Building Society in the UK, Banca Carige in Italy, and numerous others, have turned to their mainframes and DB2 for z/OS to support mobile initiatives. Mainframe solutions not only provide robust security and high performance, they are already the repositories for much of the data that mobile applications can use. DB2 for z/OS, for example, has supported geo-location information with its built in "spatial" support for many years. It is continually evolving and adapting to support the latest technology paradigms and standards such as RESTful APIs, JSON, BSON, and others. These capabilities, along with the high reliability, availability, and security qualities of service make your mainframe the ideal database and operating environment for mobile solutions.

Case study: Reducing costs and accelerating time to value with analytics and mobile on the mainframe

As banking customers increasingly embrace Web and mobile technologies, their expectations for 24 x 7 service are growing. For Banca Carige, this raised the stakes for ensuring round-the-clock availability for its digital channels.

Business challenge: Needed to develop an improved understanding of consumer behavior through analytics, and launch new mobile services that engage and retain customers through great service.

Business solution: Built an analytics environment and a new mobile banking service using IBM software on IBM mainframes, which are designed to provide continuous availability and high security.

Business outcome: Launching new services meets changing customer demands, while the proven underlying technology accelerates deployment and reduces risk; consolidating to a single platform cuts cost and complexity.

"System reliability is becoming more and more important as customers move away from the traditional model of in-branch banking," comments Daniele Cericola, ICT Governance Manager, Banca Carige. "In developing our new mobile capabilities, the obvious choice was to run the key components on the mainframe to ensure availability." While the front end of Banca Carige's new mobile application currently runs in the cloud, it connects back into Web services running on IBM WebSphere® on Linux on the z Systems platform. Transactions and queries that are initiated on the mobile channel are ultimately processed through CICS and DB2 on the mainframe.

> Unavailability of systems, applications, or data, whether intentional or unintentional, has huge financial implications such as lost business, brand damage, and penalties, particularly for financial situations. In late 2014, an outage at a UK bank was hit with a GBP56 million fine. The Bank of England and Financial Conduct Authority issued the fine because 6.5 million customers were unable to make payments for as much as three weeks.
>
> The bank had already paid out more than GBP70 million in compensation to customers, in addition to cutting bonuses for thousands of staff responsible. The bank has spent more than GBP500 million on bolstering defenses against a similar future outage.

The Need for Speed, Data Currency, and Security

Today's banking customers demand the most up-to-date information, expecting to see transactions made a few seconds ago reflected on their accounts almost instantly. The same impatience applies to mobile users who can and will move on if delays last even a few seconds. Your platform must be capable of accelerating customer response times quickly and easily—giving answers and insights faster. Mobile customers won't settle for stale, cached, or warehoused data replicas.

What's more, slow performance can also leave the bank open to potential fraud. Banks in particular demand the toughest data security and operational resilience capabilities if they expect to attract new customers and retain existing ones with assurances that every customer's data is safe. Data breaches and unavailability of systems have cost banks billions of dollars in fines along with brand damage and major trust issues from customers who are asking, "Why would I want to do business with a company that can't even protect my data?"

The bottom line is that your organization's ability to use mobile computing to build business is directly dependent on your ability to manage your big data smarter. To meet user demands, the organization must provide the highest possible quality of service, often prioritizing mobile transactions to make sure you deliver in the "mobile moment."

DB2 for z/OS is not only the world's premier data store for transactions but also the core of the modern enterprise central data warehouse that today's advanced analytics require. Acceleration technologies such as IBM DB2 Analytics Accelerator for z/OS can slash query times from days to just seconds, making real-time analytics possible on mobile transactions. These levels of performance, scalability, and security are indispensable for creating a mobile channel that is attractive and useful for customers, partners, and employees alike. For banks and many other industries, IBM z Systems with DB2 for z/OS can help deliver lower costs, lower risks, and more opportunities for growing market share and profitability. Successful mobile banking initiatives require organizations to be capable of performing real-time analytics on mobile transactions to detect and correlate events. When your organization has access to the insights produced by analytics, you then have the information you need to help improve operations and drive new business opportunities.

Under the Hood of a Secure and Fraud-Resistant Mobile Transaction

The world has become a smaller place due in large measure to cell phones moving with users wherever they go. Legitimate transactions can occur at any time of the day—in an airplane 38,000 feet above an ocean or from multiple transactions on the same device in different continents within a few hours. This behavior makes detecting fraud even more challenging.

Consider a banking funds transfer transaction involving DB2 for z/OS and CICS shown in Figure 1. The scenario is based on helping to detect fraud that might occur during a mobile transaction. All of this has to happen in near real-time, whether the customer is looking up an account balance, transferring funds, paying a bill, or purchasing an item.

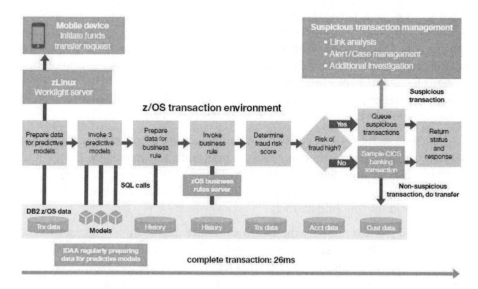

Figure 1: How a mobile transaction can be analyzed for potential fraud

To help spot potential fraud, sophisticated predictive models are used and continually refined. In order to achieve the best models, the process shown above needs to be fed by the results of highly complex queries looking at a large number of variables. These can include the account history of the customer; their geographic locations in the last hour, two hours, day, couple of days, week, or month; the customer's current balance and credit rating; the mobile device they are using; whether the interaction is outside of usual behavioral patterns; and many other parameters.

The analysis of these variables using IBM SPSS® software can help predict the probability of fraud with identified degrees of confidence and determine whether or not to allow the transaction to occur. All of what's shown in Figure 1 is happening in 26ms or less on an IBM zEnterprise® 196 mainframe. Prior to the introduction of the analytics accelerator, these models might be refreshed with data as infrequently as once a week because of the complex nature of the queries and analysis needed to feed the models. This frequency would leave the process open to potential fraud because models are being fed with old data. Now, with the analytics accelerator deployed, the models can be updated every day or even more frequently. By updating data faster and more often, the models can be adapted and refined constantly to help reduce the risk of fraud.

Reuse Services and Data to Build Portable Mobile Apps

Given all that's been discussed so far, how can an organization like a bank build mobile apps that ensure the right levels of function while maintaining the tightest security controls?

One of the key requirements is simplifying controlled access to functions within existing back-end services as well as to data used and stored in databases such as DB2 for z/OS. Many customers would like to leverage their trusted investments into IBM z Systems by reusing and exposing existing business logic and transactions, and combining this data with new features in a mobile application. They would also like to open up some of the functions as consumable services or both internal and public APIs.

While simplicity is a key element, all of this must be completed at an enterprise-grade level. That means taking into account the requirements of security, control, monitoring, traceability, and serviceability. Also needed is a common way to interact with all z/OS business and infrastructure assets using the key standards employed in mobile application development such as RESTful APIs, JSON, BSON and Mongo APIs.

Reducing the Complexity of Multiple Mobile Platform Support

While mobile is attractive as a channel, it can also bring numerous challenges if the right application development and infrastructure is not in place.

Mobile devices are often shared between family members or coworkers, so identification of the individual using a particular device is important. Mobile devices themselves also have multiple personas—some are used for personal entertainment while others are used as corporate devices. In addition, some scenarios could include personal devices that are also configured for use at corporate locations.

Furthermore, there is a wide variety of operating systems at various levels of maturity. Each of these varieties and their communications service providers need to be supported. Otherwise, your mobile channel could exclude a huge segment of your bank's potential customer market.

In most cases, mobile transactions receive a high priority because organizations know the mobile channel is often used in impulse buying situations. For that reason, a consistent and exceptional customer experience must be maintained at all times. The IBM MobileFirst™ Platform enables developers to build and continuously deliver mobile apps more efficiently and effectively. The platform extends on the development, delivery, and management capabilities of IBM MobileFirst Platform Foundation (formerly IBM

Worklight®), providing a comprehensive mobile application development solution.

The result is an integrated platform that can accelerate the delivery of your mobile strategy with increased productivity and security while providing users with a more engaging experience. z/OS Connect can be used within IBM MobileFirst Platform or as standalone software within other vendors' development environments, as shown in Figure 2.

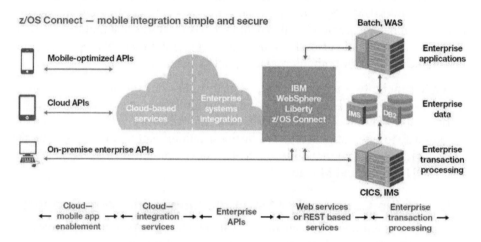

Figure 2: z/OS Connect enables connectivity between the mobile environment and back-end z/OS systems.

z/OS Connect is a unified solution for cloud, mobile, and Web integration. It offers service enablement, management, discovery and secure access to z/OS assets. IBM Information Management System (IMS™) Connect offers TCP access to the IBM IMS transaction manager and database systems. From a DB2 for z/OS perspective, IBM has created access via JSON, the most widely used protocol and language for developing mobile apps. JSON is a language-independent data format with readily available code for parsing and generating JSON data in a large variety of programming languages (see Figure 3).

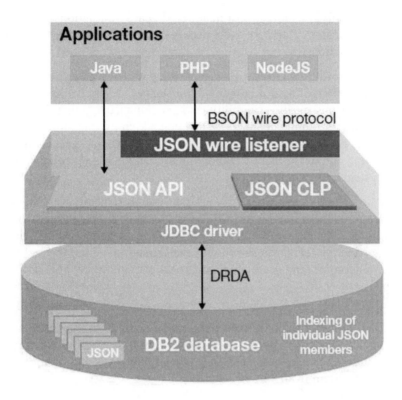

Figure 3: JSON is a popular protocol that can be used access z/OS assets.

Developers can also write applications using Mongo APIs as if they are communicating with a Mongo database. However, they are in fact directly accessing data stored in DB2 for z/OS. This is important because MongoDB is currently one of the most popular implementations of a NoSQL database used extensively by mobile apps.

This represents the best of both worlds:

- Fully supported Mongo APIs
- Industrial-strength, security, scalability, and availability of DB2 for z/OS

IBM z Systems—Designed for the Mobile Era

Global organizations of all types—including 92 of the world's top 100 banks, 23 of the top 25 US retailers, and nine of the world's 10 largest insurance organizations—trust their business to securable, scalable, self-optimizing IBM z Systems mainframes.[5] Estimates are, in fact, that despite the growth of distributed computing, mainframes still process roughly 30 billion business transactions daily, including most major credit card transactions, stock trades, and money transfers.[6] DB2 for z/OS data is likely to be involved in the majority of these interactions.

In other words, data infrastructures running on IBM z Systems are already used as the system of record in many organizations. Many banks are finding the system's built-in security, scalability, and performance together form an ideal infrastructure for mobile channels. When you add in the capabilities for big data analysis and cost efficient mobile channels, z Systems are well suited for transforming enterprise mobile computing to interact more profitably with end users' systems of engagement.

As the system of record, z Systems mainframes typically hold the latest, most accurate, up-to-the-second information that can help drive enterprise business decisions for engaging with users and influencing user actions via their mobile devices. The z Systems infrastructure is well suited to deliver the real-time mobile transactions and access to mobile data that both users and organizations demand.

IBM mainframes based on z/OS are designed to cope with the increased unpredictability of workloads created by mobile computing. As IBM has defined and extended mainframe capabilities, IBM z Systems, for example, now support nearly 5,000 MIPS in a single footprint—nearly 10 times the capabilities of a z/OS-based system from 10 years ago.[7]

Case study: Growing the business with a secure multi-channel business

The Nationwide Building Society in the UK is the world's largest building society. It was established over 160 years ago, serves over 14 million members, and is still growing.

Business challenge: Nationwide knew that it needed to transform its service offerings to embrace new channels and personalized products. Customers demanded an always-on, multi-channel banking system.

Business solution: Used DB2 for z/OS to enable to operate in real time and across multiple channels with resiliency and stability for managing millions of accounts. Used IBM security tools to manage different levels of access rights with ease.

Business outcome: 24 x 7 availability to support anytime, anywhere banking services, shorter time-to-market for new accounts, and ample scalability to support Nationwide's ambitious growth plans.

Conclusion

The pervasiveness of smart mobile devices has created a tipping point for many organizations, especially banks. Mobile access allows customers to do business anytime, anywhere on any device. It has driven consumers to expect, even demand, instant access to information and services. From a business perspective, organizations are beginning to leverage this always-on channel to build deep digital business relationships with their consumers, and are capitalizing on the "mobile moment" by influencing buyer decisions. IBM z Systems, and in particular DB2 for z/OS 11, are engineered to handle unexpected and unpredictable events while causing little or no negative impact on existing workloads. What's more, new mobile pricing models make z Systems an even more cost-effective and appealing business decision than before.

IBM DB2 for z/OS can deliver great value and significant benefits for a mobile initiative, especially for financial institutions. With enhanced security and simplified access to back-end data and services, z Systems mainframes can integrate with the IBM MobileFirst Platform as well as many other development platforms that use open standards. With this dynamic, ground-breaking z Systems software, you can create an effective mobile channel faster and simpler to help you get a first-mover competitive advantage. If your goals are to lower business costs, reduce business risks, and gain a competitive advantage, IBM DB2 for z/OS is an ideal choice for your mobile needs.

For More Information

For more information, visit *ibm.com/software/data/db2/zos/family/*.

Notes

1. Montez, Tiffani. "The State of North American Digital and Multichannel Banking 2013." Forrester Research Inc. (April 2, 2013)

2. "VNI Mobile Forecast 2013-2018." Cisco Systems.

3. "VNI Mobile Forecast." Cisco.

4. These claims are based on results from IBM internal lab measurements and projections.

5. Sun, Janet L. "Don't Believe the Myth—information about the Mainframe." http://www.share.org/p/bl/et/blogid=2&blogaid=234 (May, 2013)

6. Sun. "Don't Believe the Myth—information about the Mainframe."

7. Based on preliminary internal measurements and projections and compared to the z114 and/or z10 BC. Official performance data will be available upon announcement. Results may vary by customer based on individual workload, configuration, and software levels. Visit LSPR website for more details at *ibm.com/servers/resourcelink/lib03060.nsf/pages/lsprindex?OpenDocument*.

DB2 for z/OS and Spark Integration

DB2 and Spark—the Perfect Partner for Big Data

by Pallavi Priyadarshini

Introduction: What Is Spark?

Apache® Spark™ is an open source cluster computing framework with in-memory processing to speed analytic applications up to 100 times faster compared to technologies on the market today. Developed in the AMPLab at UC Berkeley, Apache Spark can help reduce data interaction complexity, increase processing seed and enhance mission-critical applications with deep intelligence.

Highly versatile in many environments, Apache Spark is known for its ease of use in creating algorithms that harness insight from complex data. Spark was elevated to a top-level Apache Project in 2014 and continues to expand today.

IBM is committing to the Apache Spark project with investments in design-led innovation and broad-scale education programs to promote open source innovation and accelerate intelligence into every application.

IBM and Apache Spark: The Start of Something Big in Data and Design

It's not just about data access anymore. It's about building algorithms that put analytics into action. It's about changing data science and driving intelligent apps fueled by data. Combining data, design, and speed, IBM and Apache Spark are creating a new blueprint of innovation.

Apache Spark and DB2 for z/OS

Apache Spark promises to be a game changer for Big Data and particularly DB2 for z/OS by providing a unified analytics platform and is emerging as a de-facto "analytics operating system." The Spark ecosystem is continuously growing with different products in Big Data space leveraging Spark as their underlying execution engine. Spark has quickly evolved into the hottest open source project due to its potential to solve complex Big Data problems in a very simple way: it cuts through the complexity of MapReduce and provides developer-friendly

Scala, Java, Python, and R APIs suited for both interactive and batch processing. It also provides rich libraries for machine learning, streaming, graph processing, and statistical analysis.

Because of its ability to support a wide variety of structured and unstructured data sources, Spark is positioned to be the enterprise-wide analytics engine. Most enterprises store data in heterogeneous environments with a mix of data sources. With Spark, it has become easier than ever to ingest data from disparate data sources and perform fast in-memory analytics on data combined from multiple sources, giving a 360-degree view of enterprise-wide data.

Big Data is not all about unstructured data. In fact, most real-world problems are solved using some form of structured or semi-structured data. Since DB2 is the preferred system of record for structured data, an integration of Spark with DB2 is an obvious next step in the evolution of Big Data. Enterprises store petabytes of transactional data in DB2 and run their mission-critical applications on that data. Customers often have a need to perform analytics on not just pure DB2 data, but aggregate DB2 data with other data sources to derive additional business insights. For example, a business may want to aggregate transactional data in DB2 with social media data such as Twitter data stored in Hadoop Distributed File System (HDFS) to establish patterns on consumer sentiment and take actions such as offering targeted discounts. Combining Spark and DB2 simplifies integration of mission-critical transaction data with contextual data from other sources to derive additional Big Data insights.

Spark provides an easy integration with structured data using SparkSQL—a new module in Apache Spark that integrates relational processing with Spark's functional programming API. Spark SQL Data Sources support makes it simple to connect to relational databases, load data into Spark, and also access Spark data as if it were stored in a relational database. It compiles SQL queries into a series of calls to the Spark API. SparkSQL lets Spark programmers leverage the benefits of relational processing and lets SQL users call complex analytics libraries in Spark (e.g., machine learning).

Spark, which is built with Scala, enables large-scale data processing by abstracting data as collection of objects called Resilient Distributed Datasets (RDDs) distributed across clusters. Recently Spark introduced an extension to RDD as part of SparkSQL called DataFrames—which enriches RDDs with schema, making it easier for data engineers and scientists to work with large data sets. DataFrames can be thought of as in-memory relational tables, making it easier for people who are familiar with SQL to perform analyses with Spark.

SparkSQL is viewed as the unified way to access structured data in the Spark ecosystem. DataFrames support a wide variety of data formats out of the box, such as JSON and Hive. DataFrames can also read and write to external relational data sources through the JDBC interface. This ability of DataFrames to support a wide variety of data sources and formats enables rich federation of data across many sources.

DB2 offers integration with Spark SQL using the DB2 Connect JDBC connector. The DataFrames API allows loading of DB2 data into Spark through the JDBC driver and makes it possible to easily expose DB2 data as Spark DataFrames. SQL queries can be run on a DataFrame instantiated with DB2 data. DataFrames also provides abstraction for selecting columns, joining of different data sources, aggregation, and filtering. Once DB2 data is loaded into Spark as DataFrames, this data can be joined with data from other sources, or transformations can be applied to generate new DataFrames. Transformed DataFrames can even be written back into DB2 and persisted. All this can be done via SQL, or rich language bindings in Python, Scala, Java, and R. Data scientists can go beyond joins, aggregation, and filtering on DataFrames created from DB2 data. They can even use complex user functions on DataFrames for advanced analytics as well as MLib's machine learning pipeline API for machine learning, as Figure 1 shows.

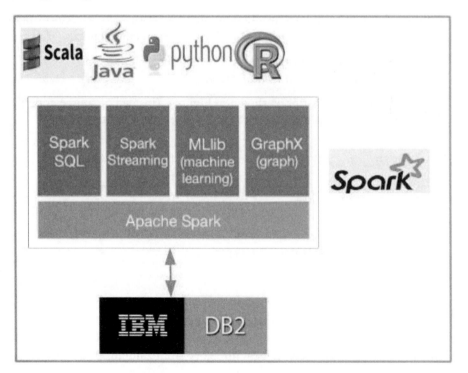

Figure 1: Overview of data integration with Apache Spark

We have a series of blog posts available on the World of DB2 to get you up and running with DB2 and Spark. These blogs also have code snippets highlighting the ease with which you can read DB2 data into Spark, persist Spark DataFrames into DB2 and use Spark to join DB2 data with other data sources such as JSON. Integration with SparkSQL enables database developers to create and run Spark programs faster, with less code. Following are the links and contents of the relevant blogs.

Blog 1: Using Spark's Interactive Scala Shell for Accessing DB2 Data Using JDBC Driver and Spark's New DataFrames API

www.worldofdb2.com/profiles/blogs/using-spark-s-interactive-scala-shell-for-accessing-db2-data

Currently the Spark shell is available in Scala and Python. This article covers accessing and filtering DB2 data via the Scala shell using the DB2-supplied JDBC driver (IBM Data Server Driver for JDBC and SQLJ). Below are the step-by-step instructions.

1. Confirm that you have Java installed by running `java -version` from a Windows command line. JDK version 1.7 or 1.8 is recommended.

2. Install Spark on the local machine by downloading Spark from *https://spark.apache.org/downloads.html*.

3. We chose pre-built binaries as shown in Figure 2 (instead of source code download) to avoid building Spark in an early-experimentation phase.

Download Spark

The latest release of Spark is Spark 1.3.1, released on April 17, 2015 (release notes) (git tag)

1. Choose a Spark release: 1.3.1 (Apr 17 2015) ▾

2. Choose a package type: Pre-built for Hadoop 2.6 and later ▾

3. Choose a download type: Direct Download ▾

4. Download Spark: spark-1.3.1-bin-hadoop2.6.tgz

5. Verify this release using the 1.3.1 signatures and checksums.

Figure 2: Downloading Spark

4. Unzip the installation file to a local directory (for example, `C:/spark`).

5. Start a Windows command prompt.

6. Navigate to the directory that has the `bin` folder of the Spark installation (`c:/spark/bin`).

7. Download the DB2 JDBC driver jar (`db2jcc.jar` or `db2jcc4.jar`) from *www-01.ibm.com/support/docview.wss?uid=swg21385217* into C:\ or any other location you choose.

8. Set `spark_classpath` to the location of the DB2 driver by running `SET SPARK_CLASSPATH=c:\db2jcc.jar`. Also include the DB2 Connect license file `db2jcc_license_cisuz.jar` if connecting to DB2 z/OS.

9. Run the `spark-shell.cmd` script found in the `bin` folder to start the Spark shell using Scala.

10. If the installation was successful, you should see output like that in Figure 3, followed by a Scala prompt, as in Figure 4.

```
15/06/02 16:40:38 INFO Server: jetty-8.y.z-SNAPSHOT
15/06/02 16:40:38 INFO AbstractConnector: Started SocketConnector@0.0.0.0:49827
15/06/02 16:40:38 INFO Utils: Successfully started service 'HTTP class server' o
n port 49827.
Welcome to



                            version 1.3.1


Using Scala version 2.10.4 (Java HotSpot(TM) Client VM, Java 1.8.0_45)
Type in expressions to have them evaluated.
```

Figure 3: A successful Spark installation

```
ost:49860 with 267.3 MB RAM, BlockManagerId(<driver>, localhost, 49860)
15/06/02 16:40:42 INFO BlockManagerMaster: Registered BlockManager
15/06/02 16:40:42 INFO SparkILoop: Created spark context..
Spark context available as sc.
15/06/02 16:40:42 INFO SparkILoop: Created sql context (with Hive support)..
SQL context available as sqlContext.

scala>
```

Figure 4: Scala prompt

11. In Figure 4, you see two important objects are already created for you:

- `SparkContext`—Any Spark application needs a `SparkContext`, which tells Spark how to access a cluster. In the shell mode, a `SparkContext` is already created for you in a variable called `sc`.

- `SqlContext`—This is needed to construct DataFrames (equivalent to relational tables) from database data and serves as the entry point for working with structured data.

12. Once you have Spark up and running, you can issue queries to DB2 on z/OS as well as DB2 for Linux, UNIX, and Windows (DB2 for LUW) through

the DB2 JDBC driver. Tables from DB2 database can be loaded as a DataFrame, using the following options on load:

- url—The JDBC URL to connect to
- dbtable—The JDBC table that should be read. Note that anything that is valid in a 'FROM' clause of a SQL query can be used.
- driver—The class name of the JDBC driver needed to connect to this URL

13. From a Scala command line, issue the following command:

```
val employeeDF = sqlContext.load("jdbc", Map("url" ->
"jdbc:db2://localhost:50000/sample:currentSchema=
pallavipr;user=pallavipr;password=XXXXXX;","driver" ->
"com.ibm.db2.jcc.DB2Driver","dbtable" ->
"pallavipr.employee"))
```

14. You should see output containing the table metadata as shown in Figure 5:

```
scala> val employeeDF = sqlContext.load("jdbc", Map("url" -> "jdbc:db2://localho
st:50000/sample:currentSchema=pallavipr;user=pallavipr;password=        ;","driv
er" -> "com.ibm.db2.jcc.DB2Driver","dbtable" -> "pallavipr.employee"))
employeeDF: org.apache.spark.sql.DataFrame = [EMPNO: string, FIRSTNME: string, M
IDINIT: string, LASTNAME: string, WORKDEPT: string, PHONENO: string, HIREDATE: d
ate, JOB: string, EDLEVEL: int, SEX: string, BIRTHDATE: date, SALARY: decimal(10
,0), BONUS: decimal(10,0), COMM: decimal(10,0)]
```

Figure 5: Table metadata

15. To see the contents of the EMPLOYEE table, issue employeeDF.show() from a Scala command line, which shows the contents of the DataFrame as captured in Figure 6. Show() returns the first 20 records from the table by default (out of about 40 existing rows).

```
EMPNO  FIRSTNME   MIDINIT LASTNAME  WORKDEPT PHONENO HIREDATE    JOB       EDLE
SEX BIRTHDATE  SALARY     BONUS    COMM
000010 CHRISTINE I         HAAS       A00      11      1995-01-01 PRES       18
F    1963-08-24 152750.00 1000.00 4220.00
000020 MICHAEL   L         THOMPSON  B01      3476    2003-10-10 MANAGER     18
M    1978-02-02 94250.00  800.00  3300.00
000030 SALLY     A         KWAN       C01      4738    2005-04-05 MANAGER     20
F    1971-05-11 98250.00  800.00  3060.00
000050 JOHN      B         GEYER      E01      6789    1979-08-17 MANAGER     16
M    1955-09-15 80175.00  800.00  3214.00
000060 IRVING    F         STERN      D11      6423    2003-09-14 MANAGER     16
M    1975-07-07 72250.00  500.00  2580.00
000070 EVA       D         PULASKI    D21      7831    2005-09-30 MANAGER     16
F    2003-05-26 96170.00  700.00  2893.00
000090 EILEEN    W         HENDERSON E11      5498    2000-08-15 MANAGER     16
F    1971-05-15 89750.00  600.00  2380.00
000100 THEODORE  Q         SPENSER    E21      0972    2000-06-19 MANAGER     14
M    1980-12-18 86150.00  500.00  2092.00
000110 VINCENZO  G         LUCCHESSI A00      3490    1988-05-16 SALESREP   19
M    1959-11-05 66500.00  900.00  3720.00
000120 SEAN                O'CONNELL A00      2167    1993-12-05 CLERK      14
M    1972-10-18 49250.00  600.00  2340.00
000130 DELORES   M         QUINTANA  C01      4578    2001-07-28 ANALYST    16
F    1955-09-15 73800.00  500.00  1904.00
000140 HEATHER   A         NICHOLLS  C01      1793    2006-12-15 ANALYST    18
F    1976-01-19 68420.00  600.00  2274.00
000150 BRUCE               ADAMSON    D11      4510    2002-02-12 DESIGNER   16
M    1977-05-17 55280.00  500.00  2022.00
000160 ELIZABETH R         PIANKA     D11      3782    2006-10-11 DESIGNER   17
F    1980-04-12 62250.00  400.00  1780.00
000170 MASATOSHI J         YOSHIMURA D11      2890    1999-09-15 DESIGNER   16
M    1981-01-05 44680.00  500.00  1974.00
000180 MARILYN   S         SCOUTTEN  D11      1682    2003-07-07 DESIGNER   17
F    1979-02-21 51340.00  500.00  1707.00
000190 JAMES     H         WALKER     D11      2986    2004-07-26 DESIGNER   16
M    1982-06-25 50450.00  400.00  1636.00
000200 DAVID               BROWN      D11      4501    2002-03-03 DESIGNER   16
M    1971-05-29 57740.00  600.00  2217.00
000210 WILLIAM   T         JONES      D11      0942    1998-04-11 DESIGNER   17
M    2003-02-23 68270.00  400.00  1462.00
000220 JENNIFER  K         LUTZ       D11      0672    1998-08-29 DESIGNER   18
F    1978-03-19 49840.00  600.00  2387.00

scala>
```

Figure 6: Contents of the EMPLOYEE table

16. You can further narrow the above search results by using filter criteria. For
    example, if you want to see only columns employee id, firstname,
    lastname, and job title out of all existing columns, you would issue
    the following command:

```
employeeDF.select("empno","firstnme","lastname","job").show()
```

This gives the results shown in Figure 7.

```
empno    firstnme   lastname    job
000010 CHRISTINE HAAS        PRES
000020 MICHAEL   THOMPSON    MANAGER
000030 SALLY     KWAN        MANAGER
000050 JOHN      GEYER       MANAGER
000060 IRVING    STERN       MANAGER
000070 EVA       PULASKI     MANAGER
000090 EILEEN    HENDERSON MANAGER
000100 THEODORE  SPENSER     MANAGER
000110 VINCENZO  LUCCHESSI SALESREP
000120 SEAN      O'CONNELL CLERK
000130 DELORES   QUINTANA    ANALYST
000140 HEATHER   NICHOLLS    ANALYST
000150 BRUCE     ADAMSON     DESIGNER
000160 ELIZABETH PIANKA      DESIGNER
000170 MASATOSHI YOSHIMURA DESIGNER
000180 MARILYN   SCOUTTEN    DESIGNER
000190 JAMES     WALKER      DESIGNER
000200 DAVID     BROWN       DESIGNER
000210 WILLIAM   JONES       DESIGNER
000220 JENNIFER  LUTZ        DESIGNER

scala>
```

Figure 7: Search results using a filter

17. Now if you want to filter out only those rows that have job title DESIGNER, issue the following command from the Scala shell:

```
employeeDF.filter(employeeDF("job").equalTo("DESIGNER")).show()
```

You will see the results shown in Figure 8.

```
EMPNO  FIRSTNME  MIDINIT LASTNAME  WORKDEPT PHONENO HIREDATE   JOB       EDLEVEL
SEX BIRTHDATE  SALARY    BONUS   COMM
000150 BRUCE             ADAMSON   D11       4510    2002-02-12 DESIGNER 16
M   1977-05-17 55280.00 500.00 2022.00
000160 ELIZABETH R       PIANKA    D11       3782    2006-10-11 DESIGNER 17
F   1980-04-12 62250.00 400.00 1780.00
000170 MASATOSHI J       YOSHIMURA D11       2890    1999-09-15 DESIGNER 16
M   1981-01-05 44680.00 500.00 1974.00
000180 MARILYN   S       SCOUTTEN  D11       1682    2003-07-07 DESIGNER 17
F   1979-02-21 51340.00 500.00 1707.00
000190 JAMES     H       WALKER    D11       2986    2004-07-26 DESIGNER 16
M   1982-06-25 50450.00 400.00 1636.00
000200 DAVID             BROWN     D11       4501    2002-03-03 DESIGNER 16
M   1971-05-29 57740.00 600.00 2217.00
000210 WILLIAM   T       JONES     D11       0942    1998-04-11 DESIGNER 17
M   2003-02-23 68270.00 400.00 1462.00
000220 JENNIFER  K       LUTZ      D11       0672    1998-08-29 DESIGNER 18
F   1978-03-19 49840.00 600.00 2387.00
200170 KIYOSHI           YAMAMOTO D11       2890    2005-09-15 DESIGNER 16
M   1981-01-05 64680.00 500.00 1974.00
200220 REBA      K       JOHN      D11       0672    2005-08-29 DESIGNER 18
F   1978-03-19 69840.00 600.00 2387.00
```

Figure 8: Results of additional filtering

Blog 2: Accessing DB2 Data from Spark via Standalone Scala/Java Programs in Eclipse

www.worldofdb2.com/profiles/blogs/accessing-db2-data-via-standalone-scala-java-programs-in-eclipse

This second article focuses on accessing DB2 data via standalone Scala and Java programs in Eclipse using the DB2 JDBC driver and the DataFrames API. Following are the detailed step-by-step instructions. Note that same instructions will apply to DB2 on all platforms (z/OS, LUW, i) as well as Informix.

1. Confirm that you have Java installed by running `java -version` from a Windows command line. JDK version 1.7 or 1.8 is recommended.

2. Install Spark on the local machine by downloading Spark from *https://spark.apache.org/downloads.html*.

3. We chose pre-built binaries, as shown in Figure 9 (instead of source code download), to avoid building Spark in an early-experimentation phase.

Download Spark

The latest release of Spark is Spark 1.3.1, released on April 17, 2015 (release notes) (git tag)

1. Choose a Spark release: 1.3.1 (Apr 17 2015) ▼

2. Choose a package type: Pre-built for Hadoop 2.6 and later   ▼

3. Choose a download type: Direct Download ▼

4. Download Spark: spark-1.3.1-bin-hadoop2.6.tgz

5. Verify this release using the 1.3.1 signatures and checksums.

Figure 9: Downloading Spark

4. Unzip the installation file to a local directory (for example, `C:/spark`).

5. Download the Scala Eclipse IDE from *scala-ide.org/download/sdk.html*.

6. Unzip `scala-SDK-4.1.0-vfinal-2.11-win32.win32.x86_64.zip` into a folder (for example, `c:\Eclipse_Scala`).

7. Find `eclipse.exe` in the eclipse folder and run it. Make sure you have 64-bit Java installed, by running `java -version` from a command prompt. Incompatibility between the 64-bit Eclipse package and 32-bit Java will result in an error; if this occurs, Eclipse will not start.

8. Choose a workspace for your Scala project, as shown in Figure 10.

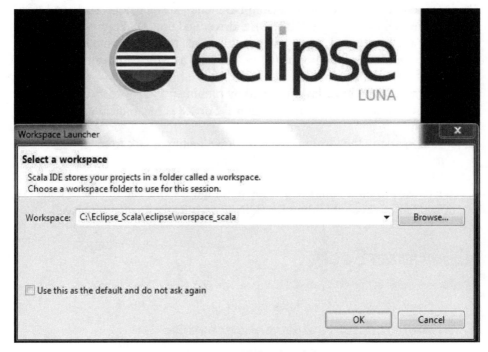

Figure 10: Choosing a workspace

9. Create a new Scala project by selecting **File** > **New Scala Project**.

10. Add the Spark libraries downloaded in step 3 to the newly created Scala project, as shown in Figure 11.

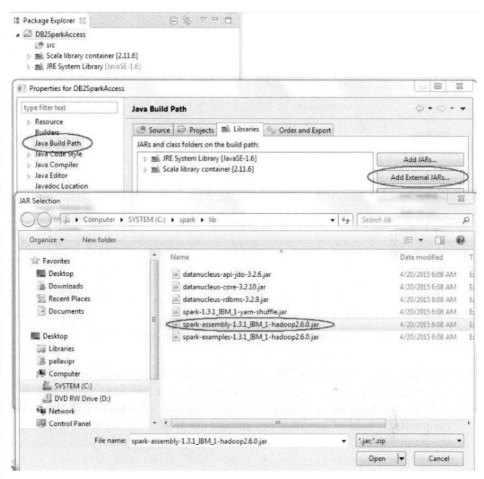

Figure 11: Adding the Spark libraries to the Scala project

11. Because Spark has its own copy of the Scala library, you may see the error message "more than one scala library found in the build path ...," as shown in Figure 12.

Figure 12: Error message

12. To remove the error, remove the Scala reference from the Java build path, as shown in Figure 13.

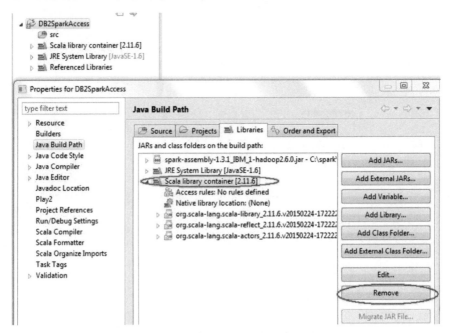

Figure 13: Removing the Scala reference from the Java build path

13. You may see another error "The version of scala library found in the build path of DB2SparkAccess (2.10.4) is prior to the one provided by scala IDE (2.11.6). Setting a Scala Installation Choice to match." **Right-click Project > Properties > Scala Compiler** and change the project setting to 2.10, as shown in Figure 14.

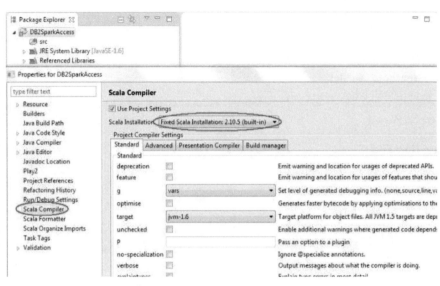

Figure 14: Changing the project setting to 2.10

14. After you **click** OK, the project will be rebuilt. You'll see only a warning about different Scala versions; ignore this warning.

15. Now you can **right-click** the DB2SparkAccess project and choose New Scala App, as shown in Figure 15. Enter the application name, and **click** Finish.

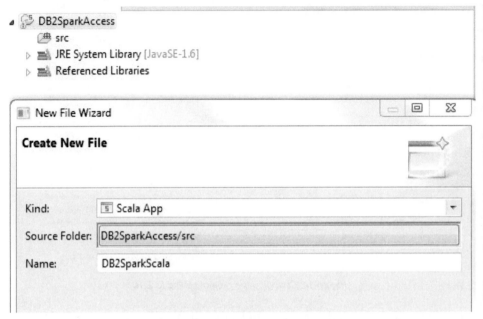

Figure 15: Creating the new Scala app

16. Copy the following source code into the new Scala application you have
    created (.scala file) and modify the database credentials so they match
    your credentials.

```
import org.apache.spark.sql.SQLContext
import org.apache.spark.SparkConf
import org.apache.spark.SparkContext

object DB2SparkScala extends App {
val conf = new SparkConf()
.setMaster("local[1]")
.setAppName("GetEmployee")
.set("spark.executor.memory", "1g")

val sc = new SparkContext(conf)

val sqlContext = new SQLContext(sc)

val employeeDF = sqlContext.load("jdbc", Map(
"url" ->
"jdbc:db2://localhost:50000/sample:currentSchema=pallavipr;user=
pallavipr;password=XXXX;",
"driver" -> "com.ibm.db2.jcc.DB2Driver",
"dbtable" -> "pallavipr.employee"))

employeeDF.show();}
```

17. **Right-click** the application and select **Run As** > **Scala application**, as
shown in Figure 16.

Figure 16: Running the Scala application

18. You may see the following exception:

```
Exception in thread "main"
java.lang.ClassNotFoundException:
com.ibm.db2.jcc.DB2Driver
```

To get rid of the above exception, select **Project** > **Properties** and configure the Java Build Path to include the IBM DB2 JDBC driver (db2jcc.jar or db2jcc4.jar), as shown in Figure 17. You can download the JDBC driver from *www-01.ibm.com/support/docview.wss?uid=swg21385217*. Also include the DB2 Connect license file db2jcc_license_cisuz.jar if you are connecting to DB2 for /OS.

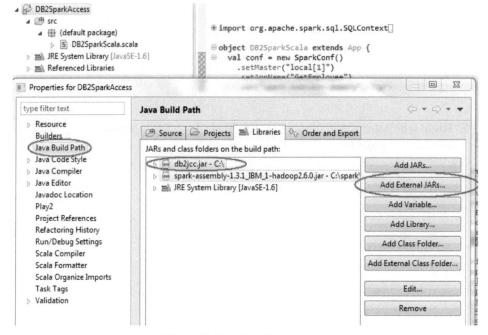

Figure 17: Removing the exception

19. Now **click** on your Scala application and select **Run As** > **Scala Application** again. You should then see the employee data retrieved from the DB2 table, as shown in Figure 18.

```
15/06/12 14:49:41 INFO MemoryStore: Block broadcast_0 of size 5296 dropped from memory (free 1126579628)
15/06/12 14:49:41 INFO BlockManager: Removing block broadcast_0_piece0
15/06/12 14:49:41 INFO MemoryStore: Block broadcast_0_piece0 of size 3381 dropped from memory (free 1126583809)
15/06/12 14:49:41 INFO BlockManagerInfo: Removed broadcast_0_piece0 on localhost:64726 in memory (size: 3.3 KB, free: 1074.4 MB)
15/06/12 14:49:41 INFO BlockManagerMaster: Updated info of block broadcast_0_piece0
EMPNO  FIRSTNME  MIDINIT LASTNAME  WORKDEPT PHONENO HIREDATE   JOB      EDLEVEL SEX BIRTHDATE  SALARY    BONUS   COMM
000010 CHRISTINE I       HAAS      A00      11      1995-01-01 PRES     18      F   1963-08-24 152750.00 1000.00 4220.00
000020 MICHAEL   L       THOMPSON  B01      3476    2003-10-10 MANAGER  18      M   1978-02-02 94250.00  800.00  3300.00
000030 SALLY     A       KWAN      C01      4738    2005-04-05 MANAGER  20      F   1971-05-11 98250.00  800.00  3060.00
000050 JOHN      B       GEYER     E01      6789    1979-08-17 MANAGER  16      M   1955-09-15 80175.00  800.00  3214.00
000060 IRVING    F       STERN     D11      6423    2003-09-14 MANAGER  16      M   1975-07-07 72250.00  500.00  2580.00
000070 EVA       D       PULASKI   D21      7831    2005-09-30 MANAGER  16      F   2003-05-26 96170.00  700.00  2893.00
000090 EILEEN    W       HENDERSON E11      5498    2000-08-15 MANAGER  16      F   1971-05-15 89750.00  600.00  2380.00
000100 THEODORE  Q       SPENSER   E21      0972    2000-06-19 MANAGER  14      M   1980-12-18 86150.00  500.00  2092.00
000110 VINCENZO  G       LUCCHESSI A00      3490    1988-05-16 SALESREP 19      M   1959-11-05 66500.00  900.00  3720.00
000120 SEAN              O'CONNELL A00      2167    1993-12-05 CLERK    14      M   1972-10-18 49250.00  600.00  2340.00
000130 DELORES   M       QUINTANA  C01      4578    2001-07-28 ANALYST  16      F   1955-09-15 73800.00  500.00  1904.00
000140 HEATHER   A       NICHOLLS  C01      1793    2006-12-15 ANALYST  18      F   1976-01-19 68420.00  600.00  2274.00
000150 BRUCE             ADAMSON   D11      4510    2002-02-12 DESIGNER 16      M   1977-05-17 55280.00  500.00  2022.00
000160 ELIZABETH R       PIANKA    D11      3782    2006-10-11 DESIGNER 17      F   1980-04-12 62250.00  400.00  1780.00
000170 MASATOSHI J       YOSHIMURA D11      2890    1999-09-15 DESIGNER 16      M   1981-01-05 44680.00  500.00  1974.00
000180 MARILYN   S       SCOUTTEN  D11      1682    2003-07-07 DESIGNER 17      F   1979-02-21 51340.00  500.00  1707.00
000190 JAMES     H       WALKER    D11      2986    2004-07-26 DESIGNER 16      M   1982-06-25 50450.00  400.00  1636.00
000200 DAVID             BROWN     D11      4501    2002-03-03 DESIGNER 16      M   1971-05-29 57740.00  600.00  2217.00
000210 WILLIAM   T       JONES     D11      0942    1998-04-11 DESIGNER 17      M   2003-02-23 68270.00  400.00  1462.00
000220 JENNIFER  K       LUTZ      D11      0672    1998-08-29 DESIGNER 18      F   1978-03-19 49840.00  600.00  2387.00
15/06/12 14:49:41 INFO ContextCleaner: Cleaned broadcast 0
getting access token
```

Figure 18: Results of running the Scala application

20. To perform a similar database access action via a standalone Java program, **click** on **Project** > **New** > **Other**, as shown in Figure 19.

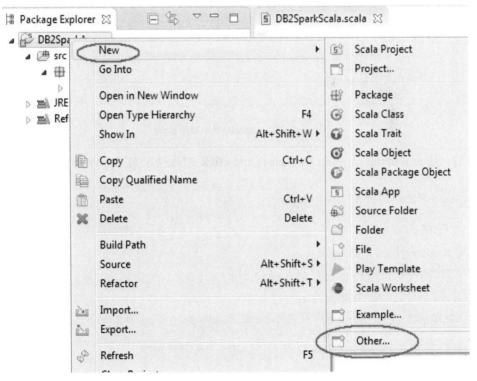

Figure 19: Database access through a standalone Java program

21. Select **Java** > **Class** and click Next; you will see a screen like Figure 20.

Figure 20: Creating the Java class

22. Enter a name for your Java class and **click** Finish, as shown in Figure 21.

Source folder:	DB2SparkAccess/src		Browse...
Package:		(default)	Browse...
☐ Enclosing type:	DB2SparkScala		Browse...
Name:	DB2SparkJava		
Modifiers:	⦿ public ○ package ○ private ○ protected		

Figure 21: Entering the Java class name

23. Paste the following code into your newly created class (. java file); change the database credentials to your credentials.

```
import java.util.HashMap;
import java.util.Map;
import org.apache.spark.SparkConf;
import org.apache.spark.api.java.JavaSparkContext;
import org.apache.spark.sql.DataFrame;
import org.apache.spark.sql.SQLContext;
public class DB2SparkJava {
public static void main(String[] args) {

SparkConf conf = new SparkConf().setAppName("Simple Application");

conf.setMaster("local[1]");
conf.set("spark.executor.memory", "1g");

JavaSparkContext sc = new JavaSparkContext(conf);

SQLContext sqlContext = new SQLContext(sc);

Map<String, String> options = new HashMap<String, String>();
options.put(
"url",
"jdbc:db2://localhost:50000/sample:currentSchema=pallavipr;user=
pallavipr;password=XXXX;");
options.put("driver", "com.ibm.db2.jcc.DB2Driver");
options.put("dbtable", "pallavipr.employee");

DataFrame jdbcDF = sqlContext.load("jdbc", options);

jdbcDF.show();}}
```

24. **Right-click** your newly created Java application. Select **Run As** > **Java application**. You should see results similar to those in step 19.

Blog 3: Simplify Joining DB2 Data and JSON Data with Spark

www.worldofdb2.com/profiles/blogs/spark-blog-3-simplify-joining-db2-data-and-json-data-with-spark

Spark SQL provides a powerful API to enable you to work with data across different data sources using Python, Scala, and Java. In this post, we will demonstrate how easily DB2 data (both z/OS and LUW) can be loaded into Spark and joined with JSON data using DataFrames.

We will use a standalone Java program in this example. For instructions on how to set up Eclipse to work with Spark, please refer to Blog 2 (page 77).

Following are the step-by-step instructions for our sample program.

1. Using the Command Line Processor (CLP), create a table in DB2 (EMPLOYEESUB) that contains a subset of EMPLOYEE information. The DDL for EMPSUB is as follows:

```
CREATE TABLE "PALLAVIPR"."EMPLOYEESUB" ( "EMPNO" CHAR(6) NOT NULL
, "FIRSTNME" VARCHAR(12) NOT NULL , "MIDINIT" CHAR(1) , "LASTNAME"
VARCHAR(15) NOT NULL , "WORKDEPT" CHAR(3) , "COMM" DECIMAL(9,2) )
```

Change the schema to your schema and make sure that you are connected to the correct database you want to create your table in. Figure 22 shows the CREATE TABLE command.

```
db2 => connect to sample

   Database Connection Information

 Database server        = DB2/NT64 10.1.2
 SQL authorization ID   = PALLAVIP...
 Local database alias   = SAMPLE

db2 => CREATE TABLE "PALLAVIPR"."EMPLOYEESUB" ( "EMPNO" CHAR(6) NOT NULL ,    "F
IRSTNME" VARCHAR(12) NOT NULL , "MIDINIT" CHAR(1) , "LASTNAME" VARCHAR(15) NOT N
ULL ,   "WORKDEPT" CHAR(3) ,   "COMM" DECIMAL(9,2) )
DB20000I  The SQL command completed successfully.
db2 =>
```

Figure 22: CREATE TABLE command in CLP

2. Load the EMPLOYEESUB table with the following five rows of data, which are stored in a comma-separated values (CSV) file (C:\1.csv). Figure 23 shows the command to do this.

```
"000010","CHRISTINE","I","HAAS","A00",+0004220.00
"000020","MICHAEL","L","THOMPSON","B01",+0003300.00
"000030","SALLY","A","KWAN","C01",+0003060.00
"000050","JOHN","B","GEYER","E01",+0003214.00
"000060","IRVING","F","STERN","D11",+0002580.00
```

```
db2 => IMPORT FROM "C:\1.csv" OF DEL METHOD P (1, 2, 3, 4, 5, 6) MESSAGES "C:\11
" INSERT INTO EMPLOYEESUB(EMPNO, FIRSTNME, MIDINIT, LASTNAME, WORKDEPT, COMM)

Number of rows read      = 6
Number of rows skipped   = 0
Number of rows inserted  = 5
Number of rows updated   = 0
Number of rows rejected  = 1
Number of rows committed = 6
```

Figure 23: Loading EMPLOYEESUB with data from a CSV file

3. Copy the following contents into a JSON file (`employeesub.json`):

```
{ "EMPNO":"000010", "EDLEVEL":"18", "SALARY":"152750.00",
"BONUS":"1000.00" }
{ "EMPNO":"000020", "EDLEVEL":"18", "SALARY":"94250.00",
"BONUS":"800.00" }
{ "EMPNO":"000030", "EDLEVEL":"20", "SALARY":"98250.00",
"BONUS":"800.00" }
{ "EMPNO":"000050", "EDLEVEL":"16", "SALARY":"80175.00",
"BONUS":"800.00" }
{ "EMPNO":"000060", "EDLEVEL":"16", "SALARY":"72250.00",
"BONUS":"500.00" }
```

4. As you can see, the DB2 table EMPLOYEESUB contains six columns:
   EMPNO, FIRSTNME, MIDINIT, LASTNAME, WORKDEPT, and COMM, while
   the JSON file has the following four keys: EMPNO, EDLEVEL, SALARY, and
   BONUS. Our goal is to join both sets of data using EMPNO as the join key, so
   that a combined data set can be created with all employee information in
   one place.

5. Copy the following program in an Eclipse `java` class:

```
 1:
 2:     import java.util.HashMap;
 3:     import java.util.Map;
 4:
 5:     import org.apache.log4j.Level;
 6:     import org.apache.log4j.Logger;
 7:     import org.apache.spark.SparkConf;
 8:     import org.apache.spark.api.java.JavaSparkContext;
 9:     import org.apache.spark.sql.DataFrame;
10:     import org.apache.spark.sql.Row;
11:     import org.apache.spark.sql.SQLContext;
12:
13:     public class DB2JsonJoinSpark {
14:       public static void main(String[] args) {
15:
16:             SparkConf conf = new SparkConf();
17:
18:             conf.setMaster("local[1]");
19:             conf.setAppName("GetUnionEmployeeTable");
20:             conf.set("spark.executor.memory", "1g");
21:
22:             String path = "C:\\Eclipse_Scala\\employeesub.json";
23:
24:             JavaSparkContext sc = new JavaSparkContext(conf);
25:             SQLContext sqlContext = new SQLContext(sc);
26:
27:             Map<String, String> options = new HashMap<String,
String>();
28:             options.put("url",
"jdbc:db2://localhost:50000/sample:currentSchema=pallavipr;user=
pallavipr;password=XXXXXX;");
29:             options.put("driver", "com.ibm.db2.jcc.DB2Driver");
30:             options.put("dbtable", "pallavipr.employeesub");
31:
32:             DataFrame df1 = sqlContext.load("jdbc", options);
33:             df1.show();
34:
35:             DataFrame df2 = sqlContext.jsonFile(path);
36:             df2.show();
37:
38:             DataFrame finaldf = df1.join(df2, df2.col("EMPNO").
equalTo(df1.col("EMPNO")) );
39:             System.out.println("Printing Joined Data");
40:             finaldf.show();
41:       }
42:     }
```

6. As shown in the previous code, we create SQLContext in line 25 to work with the RDMS and load DB2 data into Spark using the DB2 JDBC driver as a DataFrame in line 32. We load JSON data as a Spark DataFrame in line 35.

7. Make sure that you have included the Spark libraries, DB2 JDBC driver jar, and DB2 Connect license file db2jcc_license_cisuz.jar in the Build path, as shown in Figure 24.

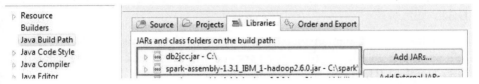

Figure 24: Build path

8. **Right-click** the Java class and **Run As Java application**. You should see the output shown in Figure 25 on the console.

```
15/08/04 18:16:03 INFO DAGScheduler: Job 4 finished: show at DB2JsonJoinSpark.java:39, took 1.407471 s
+------+---------+-------+--------+--------+-------+-------+--------+------+---------+
| EMPNO| FIRSTNME|MIDINIT|LASTNAME|WORKDEPT|   COMM|  BONUS|EDLEVEL| EMPNO|  SALARY|
+------+---------+-------+--------+--------+-------+-------+--------+------+---------+
|000060|   IRVING|      F|   STERN|     D11|2580.00| 500.00|      16|000060| 72250.00|
|000010|CHRISTINE|      I|    HAAS|     A00|4220.00|1000.00|      18|000010|152750.00|
|000020|  MICHAEL|      L|THOMPSON|     B01|3300.00| 800.00|      18|000020| 94250.00|
|000030|    SALLY|      A|    KWAN|     C01|3060.00| 800.00|      20|000030| 98250.00|
|000050|     JOHN|      B|   GEYER|     E01|3214.00| 800.00|      16|000050| 80175.00|
+------+---------+-------+--------+--------+-------+-------+--------+------+---------+

15/08/04 18:16:03 INFO SparkContext: Invoking stop() from shutdown hook
```

Figure 25: Sample application output

As you can see in Figure 25, the output contains data from both the DB2 table and JSON file, joined by EMPNO. This example clearly highlights the ease with which Spark enables join across disparate data sources with its powerful DataFrames API.

Enjoy your Spark test-drive with DB2!

Blog 4: Persisting Spark DataFrames into DB2

www.worldofdb2.com/profiles/blogs/spark-blog-4-persisting-spark-dataframes-into-db2

There are several use cases where data in Spark needs to be persisted in a back-end database. Enterprise-wide analytics may require loading of data into Spark from different data sources, applying transformations, performing in-memory analytics, and writing the transformed data back to an enterprise RDMS such as DB2.

In this blog, we demonstrate simple techniques using the latest Spark release to load data from a JSON file into Spark and write that back into DB2 using the DB2-supplied JDBC driver.

1. Download the latest pre-built Spark library (1.4.1) from *spark.apache.org/downloads.html*. With the rapid evolution in Spark, many methods in 1.3 have been deprecated, and it is best to experiment with the latest version.

2. In your Eclipse Scala IDE build path, add the Spark library, DB2 JDBC driver and DB2 Connect license file `db2jcc_license_cisuz.jar`, as shown in Figure 26.

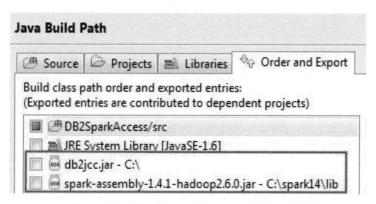

Figure 26: Adding the Spark library and DB2 JDBC driver to the build path

3. Create a `.json` file with the following contents:

```
{ "EMPNO":10, "EDLEVEL":18, "SALARY":152750, "BONUS":1000 }
  { "EMPNO":20, "EDLEVEL":18, "SALARY":94250, "BONUS":800 }
```

4. Create a Scala application with the following logic:

```
1:    val DB2_CONNECTION_URL =
"jdbc:db2://localhost:50000/sample:currentSchema=pallavipr;

user=pallavipr;password=XXXXXX;traceFile=C:/Eclipse_Scala/trace_
scala.txt;";
 2:
 3:        val conf = new SparkConf()
 4:          .setMaster("local[1]")
 5:          .setAppName("GetEmployee")
 6:          .set("spark.executor.memory", "1g")
 7:
 8:        val sc = new SparkContext(conf)
 9:        val sqlcontext = new SQLContext(sc)
10:        val path = "C:/Eclipse_Scala/empint.json"
11:
12:        val empdf = sqlcontext.read.json(path)
13:        empdf.printSchema()
14:        empdf.show()
15:
16:        Class.forName("com.ibm.db2.jcc.DB2Driver");
17:
18:        val prop = new Properties()
19:        prop.put("spark.sql.dialect" , "sql");
20:
21:        empdf.write.jdbc(DB2_CONNECTION_URL,
"PALLAVIPR.EMPLOYEESALARY", prop)
```

5. The .json file is loaded into Spark in line 12 using the new DataFrameReader introduced in Spark 1.4.0.

6. The DB2 JDBC driver is loaded in line 16 to carry out the write operation to DB2.

7. After this Scala program has been run, you will see the schema printed by the printSchema method for the DataFrame created from the .JSON file.

8. A print of the DataFrame using the Dataframe's show method produces the output shown in Figure 27.

```
+-----+--------+-----+------+
|BONUS|EDLEVEL|EMPNO|SALARY|
+-----+--------+-----+------+
| 1000|     18|   10|152750|
|  800|     18|   20| 94250|
+-----+--------+-----+------+
```

Figure 27: DataFrame output

9. The final write to DB2 is done using the `DataFrameWriter` JDBC API introduced in 1.4.0 (as shown in line 21 on page 93), which under the covers generates the `CREATE TABLE` and `INSERT` SQL statements for the EMPLOYEESALARY table.

10. You can verify that the table is created and the JSON data is inserted into DB2, as Figure 28 shows, using the tool of your choice to do so.

```
db2 => select * from employeesalary

BONUS                EDLEVEL              EMPNO                SALARY

-----                -------              -----                ------
                     1000                 18                   10                   152
750
                      800                 18                   20                    94
250

  2 record(s) selected.
```

Figure 28: Verifying table creation and insertion of JSON data

We are rapidly enhancing DB2 support in Spark to give a seamless out-of-box experience with Spark, DB2, and the DB2 JDBC driver.